ABOVE THE OVERPASS

God never wastes a heartache or a tear!

Linda Toro Stapleton

Crime Scene Photo by Lexington County,
SC Sheriff's Department

Cover Design by Tom Garber

Here I Am Publishing, LLC
780 Monterrosa Drive
Myrtle Beach, South Carolina 29572

Dedication

I was the first born of five children, so I will begin by thanking my father and my mother for my very life. They loved me more than words and gave me more than shelter and food. Their generosity and hospitality extended beyond our walls, and we always had enough. They also demonstrated a faith in someone BIGGER than themselves. They had a strong work ethic and never asked us to do something they hadn't done.

God was real in our home. Faith in Him was expected. We were all far from perfect, yet my father knelt beside me as I gave my life to Jesus at the tender age of five, a moment indelibly written on my heart and in my mind. His wisdom and knowledge of the Bible made his eyes shimmer with tender love for God.

He wrote out this verse in my first Bible:
"Study to show yourself approved unto God,
a workman that needeth not to be ashamed,
rightly dividing the WORD of truth."
(2 Timothy 2:15 KJV)

He then encouraged me to memorize it and even more of the Word so that I wouldn't sin against God. He sowed precious seeds into my life that day. We always knew Mom and Dad were praying for us. Their prayers are my treasure along with their powerful legacy of love.

Table of Contents

Dedication
Introduction
Prologue: God's Place

Introduction

In mid-summer of 1986, I had just given birth to our second child, a little girl. She joined her big brother, Will. But as a survivor of the crime that had occurred on November 5, 1986, I was barely coping with the daily routine. She was six-months-old now, and the only reason I got out of bed or even smiled again. She filled my arms and brought me comfort. But oh, how I desperately missed my active little four-year-old boy!

I would find myself standing beside my husband, Bill, in front of a full jury and packed federal courtroom in Columbia, South Carolina, as victims of a heinous crime. We were in the middle of a full-scale murder trial, reduced to mere players in a senseless tragedy, and I had no idea why or how this all happened. Our perfect, healthy, beautiful little boy was dead, gone in an instant. Two teenage boys had committed a crime so grievous that the boys were tried as adults, and the public was outraged! The loss and grief were overwhelming; life would never be the same. The battle in my head was raging and warred with my emotions.

I called myself a Christian. I had given my life to Jesus as a young child, but all of this was assaulting my theology and belief system as well. I didn't understand how a loving God could allow such an awful thing to happen. Where were the angels who were supposed to protect us? If God was love, how could this happen? Both my husband and I were painfully aware that our shameful secret before we got married brought an even deeper sense of guilt and unbearable shame and anguish. We were turning on ourselves, and it hung heavily between us. He blamed me, and I blamed myself, too. How did life get so out of control?

We were both born again believers in Christ. We traveled to many churches and did evangelistic music ministry at the time teaching and demonstrating the new way of worshipping God through choruses and contemporary music, which helped to lift noses, faces, and voices out of the traditional hymn book. We loved demonstrating the love of God through music and showing others a fresh way to worship and adore our Lord. We also believed God had forgiven us for all our past sins. But the truth was that life just did not make sense anymore. We were back to the age-old question, "Why do bad things happen to good people?"

I could forgive murderers, but I could not forgive myself. I wanted a do over! I was imploding and raging inside with an internal horror and destructive temper tantrums hidden far away. As a couple, we were both in a full battle for our sanity! I could forgive murderers, but I could not forgive my own husband. I could forgive murderers, and yet, I was so afraid that this was God's judgment for allowing all of this to happen that I could not even admit until years later that I was also mad at Him!

I was determined to take God at HIS Word, so when I heard God say, "Remember Job," on that fateful night out on I-26, November 5, 1986, I took Him at His Word. This is our "Job" story. Job is pronounced with a long "o." Everyone has an opinion, as Job's friends demonstrated, but it does not give anyone God's perspective or His mind. I already knew that Isaiah 55:8 said, *"My thoughts are not your thoughts, neither are your ways My ways"* (KJV).

I would begin a quest for understanding and peace with God that has never stopped. This is the story God wrote on my life. We walked it out together, one moment at a time.

Prologue: God's Place

The dim beam from the LED alarm clock beside my bed was my only light as I tiptoed back from a walk down the hall to my son's room. It was 3:30 in the dark of early morning, and I was awakened because I thought I had heard someone call my name. I had just looked in on our three-year old son, Will, and I stood for a few moments at the door watching his quiet, steady breathing as he was peacefully snuggled up in his blanket. Hmmm, I thought to myself, I know I heard something, . . . but I wondered what woke me. As I settled back down in the bed next to my husband, Bill, I drew the covers back up to my chin and with a bit of a shiver, closed my eyes, hoping sleep would quickly return.

A moment later I heard it again: a voice, a clear voice spoke my name: "Linda, don't be afraid." I did not feel fear at all, but what I saw did surprise me. There was a huge, magnificent being standing close to the side of the bed. I will refer to this being in the masculine because he had chiseled features, and he appeared more masculine than feminine. He was beautiful and strong, and his blonde, wavy shoulder-length hair glowed as he filled the side of the bedroom with his presence. He was wearing a glistening diamond white robe; every part of him was light and beauty.

He extended his right hand to me, and, without words or

hesitation, I took it and was immediately beside him. It was as if the blanket that covered me did not exist. I had no awareness of my physical body other than my tight grip on the being's robe. I know that I never moved my mouth or spoke out loud -- all our conversation from this point on took place only in our minds. He knew what I was thinking; I heard him speak to me inside my mind.

As we headed up and away from the world and into the darkness, he only said, "Come with me; don't let go." Since I had no intention of letting go, I relaxed a bit as I glanced back over my left shoulder. We were moving so fast I saw the whole earth becoming smaller and smaller. I clung tightly to his robe, yet I felt no speed of movement -- only joyful anticipation of where we were going.

The earth faded into a pinpoint, and as we moved through the darkness, I began to hear music, beautiful welcoming music. I have often tried to remember certain sounds. I can only compare it to an exercise in a music appreciation class to name the instruments while the music teacher played an orchestra piece. The music was soothing, inspiring, and welcoming but I could not distinguish any individual instruments Being played. In retrospect, I have to conclude that it wasn't music as we hear it, but possibly melodic voices woven together beyond what we can create or duplicate. I only know that I gave no resistance as I felt embraced and drawn into a place of feeling loved, completely and wholeheartedly!

I was filled with peace and joy and a growing sense of wonder and excitement. I was awestruck by the vastness of the Cosmos, and I felt spellbound by the beauty and light of a body of water that we were approaching. It had no end, like a winding river of the clearest crystal blue water. The glistening brilliance of the water was like a jeweler's special light that gave every ripple the appearance of floating, faceted diamonds and other gems.

As we crossed over the water, I was struck by the colors that surrounded us. The colors sang with the delight of their own music and song. The greens of the grass and the blues of the water and sky were so vibrant and pure, no filter or diffusion of light. Each blade of grass and every tree possessed a presence of life. Light was in everything, yet there was neither glare nor shadow, just a brilliance with peace and vibrancy of life with a sound all its own!

As we flew over the pasture-like countryside, fields of wild flowers seemed to wave with joy because I felt no breeze. From my vantage, I saw sheep grazing intermingled with zebra in the same area of vivid green grass. I heard and saw several distant waterfalls, and I also had a brief glimpse of a few children running and laughing as they played hide and seek near the edge of a stand of trees.

At one point, we were above a factory-like structure that emanated productivity. There were many people weaving and sewing and creating with their hands. I was not close enough to see details of what they were doing. They were in a courtyard-like space that somewhat reminded me of the sweet-grass basket weavers that sit at the ends of the marketplace in downtown Charleston. I could only see the smooth, shiny metallic-like roof to the structure below, but on the other end of the building, coming out of it was the most beautiful, white gossamer fabric that seemed to fly onto huge rolls.

At that point, I knew we were heading somewhere specific because we had only flown over the fabric factory, and we had not stopped or moved in closer to see more details. I desired to go closer to see the factory, but the being seemed on mission. There was so much to absorb. I marveled, but I never noticed any wings on the being that held my life in his large right hand. Then, in my thoughts, I wondered, *Why am I here?* The awesome being replied to my thoughts much like the deliverer of a special message would.

"You are God's servant, and your husband Bill is God's servant. You are to follow your husband because the Lord God will direct him. If you trust God's promises, you will be prosperous, you will be fruitful and multiply, and you will have great peace."

We then arrived above a courtyard and were hovering over a beautiful "Grecian-like" temple with exquisitely crafted stone work sitting upon a hill with lush vines and fragrant flowers entwined around the Corinthian columns. The floor of the courtyard below shone like highly polished white marble. A short distance away and yet at the highest elevation, was introduced and pointed out by the being as the Throne Room and residence of the Most High God. It seemed to be suspended in the sky, and yet it also seemed supported by millions of lighted wires similar to fiber optic rope lights filled with pulsing energy. The ropes of surging bright energy swirled around the base of the Throne Room as if alive, while thousands of ribbons of light and energy pulsed back and forth from below.

"Is that where God is?" I asked, and the Being replied, "Yes, HE is there."

I immediately wanted to go into the Throne Room. I was filled with a consuming desire to be in there, and I could feel the nervous excitement growing within me in anticipation of what might happen next . . . . *I am going to meet God!*

In my excitement, I asked Being, "Can I see HIM now? Please?"

He replied tersely, "No!"

I was instantly crushed, yet momentarily disappointed, because, as I lowered my head, my disappointment quickly faded as my attention was redirected from the Throne Room and drawn to the sound of many voices coming closer. I was enraptured with stunningly beautiful people approaching the Temple. It appeared to be a crowd of healthy and vibrant people in their twenties and thirties. Their countenances glowed with joy and light. Their strides were strong and purposeful as each ethnic group and nationality seemed to be represented.

Being and I hovered above the Temple courtyard. Because of my elevation, I could see they were coming from the surrounding countryside and walking up the hill toward the temple courtyard. They were all dressed in robes of delicate white gossamer fabric belted at the waist with golden rope sashes. They were laughing and talking. They would greet and hug as they met and then continue up the hill to the temple courtyard, joining in conversation with each other. They were all milling around enjoying the fellowship but clearly assembling for some event to begin.

Then I asked Being, "Why are they coming here?"

He replied, "They are gathering for a wedding."

I looked around before asking, "Where is the bride?"

In an instant, I found myself hurling back toward the earth at breakneck speed. I saw my husband sleeping peacefully next to me as I then reentered my body through the top of my head and neck. I laid there stunned. I had felt so alive, and Heaven was so real! *What had just happened?*

As I felt myself hurling toward earth, I hadn't even wanted

to come back. I wanted to stay there. Yet, here I was. The clock now said 6:15 a.m. It felt like I had only been gone moments. *Oh, why had I asked that question? Was it a dumb question? I didn't get it! What was this all about?* I shook my not a morning person husband.

"You won't believe it, Bill! I just came back from Heaven."

Bill never opened his eyes, but he did say as he rolled over, "That's good; write it down."

This supernatural excursion was just the beginning of God's preparing me for a spiritual journey that He would unfold throughout the rest of my life.

I

God's Preparation

"Why do birds suddenly appear every time you are near? Just like me, they long to be close to you."

The Carpenters

It was the early 1970s when Bill and I met as teenagers in a small-town church in southern New Jersey. Bill confessed years later he had gone home the day we met and told his mother he had found the girl he was going to marry. It wasn't quite that dramatic for me, but romance was in the air, and I was flattered by his constant attention and devotion. Steadily, we talked on the phone over the next year and paired up at church activities. My affection for him was growing, and before I knew it, even my dad would announce when he answered the phone, "Linda, it's Mr. Wonderful for you." I was in love!

As a young girl, I thought I always wanted to teach. As the oldest of five, it was not unusual for me to insist through play my younger siblings be the students while I, of course, was the teacher. I set my sights toward college, but truth be told, I just wanted to be a wife and mother. Bill, an accomplished piano and trumpet player, said he wanted to continue to pursue his music, but I knew he was more interested in pursuing me. So, by the end of the second year of college, we decided we only wanted to be together. Nothing else mattered to us than to be married and to ride the wave of young, romantic, and idealistic love. In a simple church wedding and a garden reception with red roses in full bloom, we pledged our love to each other in June of 1973, and we vowed to stay together until death parted us.

The first eight years of our marriage were full and fun, for the most part. We did all the things most young couples do except have children. We worked hard, went to church, bought a house and cars, yet in the midst of life, we felt an increasing desire to serve God in a more meaningful way. Bill sent his resume out through a Christian ministry job service, and, through a network of confirming circumstances, we rented out our house in New Jersey, packed the moving van, and said good-bye to our families. With naïve, youthful courage, we took a leap of faith that landed us in a ministry near Charleston, South Carolina. Even though the ministry job was not what we had hoped, we loved South Carolina and decided to stay and start our lives over.

We also became pregnant. We were cautious to let others know at first, but after I passed the timeline of my past three miscarriages, we told the family back in Jersey. After these nine years of marriage, we were quite excited to become parents. The months ahead were full of anticipation. I read all the books on childbirth I could get in my hands. We would take long walks down at the Battery, in and out of the lovely streets of historic Charleston, and around Folly Beach. We were planning for our future.

I was already deeply in love with the precious life growing under my heart. I did increasingly miss my family now that we were starting our own family, but Bill and I were a team and held tightly to each other. The little life planted inside of me inspired me to do the best I could. I loved every minute of being pregnant with Will. We did everything by the book, from nutrition to birthing classes. I knew I wanted a natural child birth so we chose the only birth center closest to us at that time. It was in Bamberg, South Carolina, which was almost an hour away, but it was important for both of us to have the birth with a midwife.

On a beautiful warm Sunday afternoon, December 5, 1982, I became a mother. It had been a difficult and long labor but totally behind us now as we welcomed our new little cherub. We were over the moon happy! Sunshine flooded the birth center room, as well as our souls. With Christmas coming soon, we eagerly planned on traveling north to introduce our new little guy to the family for the holidays.

Adjusting to life with a child did not come easy for us. I didn't want to make any mistakes. I wanted to do parenting right. I threw myself into my new role of Mommy with all my heart and energy. Will was the new love of my life, and even though Bill adored his new namesake, he struggled with feeling left out of the daily routine of nursing and my continual fatigue and my unavailability to him.

For us, parenting was God's way of taking two very different people and using their shared, deep love for their child to strip away the layers of self-centeredness. We loved our Lord Jesus, but in the trenches of parenting, we both were discovering new places of self-sacrifice and sharing.

Tragically, a scant four years later, our beautiful little boy would be gone in an instant. Our lives were shattered by a grief that was overwhelming; life would never be the same.

II

God's Process

"The apostles gathered around Jesus and reported to him all they had done and taught. Then, because so many people were coming and going that they did not even have a chance to eat, he said to them, 'Come with me by yourselves to a quiet place and get some rest.' So they went away by themselves in a boat to a solitary place."

Mark 6: 30-32 (NIV)

Dying to self each day was so difficult. Since Will's birth, we had pulled back from our evangelistic music ministry and tried to focus on the family. Will was sturdy, lively, and precocious. We both adored him. Bill was an involved dad, and we loved being and going places as a family. However, all the demands and pressures of the move and starting over with a young family had taken their toll on us. Even now that Will was almost four, Bill and I were still struggling with communication and intimacy issues as we were expecting a second child. Our marriage was definitely taking a back seat to parenting, and we were trying hard to recalibrate and do a better job of balancing life.

It was the summer of 1986. I was in my last month of pregnancy and feeling every degree of the South Carolina heat. I still vividly remember the one hundred-plus degree temperatures in nearby Columbia, which the evening news' meteorologist would compare to the temperatures in Death Valley, California.

We returned to the same birth center and midwife in Bamberg where we had given birth to Will. A new baby girl, Julie Lin, was born on July 21, not a minute too soon! She brought us much joy as she joined her big brother Will in being the delight of our lives. Now, with the addition of Julie Lin and more changes, adjustments, and stresses, our relationship dynamics were even more stretched. Life was overwhelming, but one thing was clear: we knew we had to get away from the heat and spend some quality time together with no noise from the demanding world. Our favorite place to relax was the mountains.

Our love for the majestic Blue Ridge Mountains had started years before our marriage while we attended college in upstate South Carolina. We would travel home on school breaks, taking the curving, winding roads with their breathtaking overlooks, and we never tired of consuming the spectacular beauty. We had purchased seventeen acres during a past vacation. Our property was located outside of Marion; the West side of it even shared a border with the Pisgah National Forest. In August, Bill had made a trip alone to move our sixteen-feet long Prowler camper trailer onto the new property, giving us a place to stay while taking our time to clear a home site. We were taking the beginning steps now that we had vision for raising our young family in a more idyllic country setting. We longed for a quiet, peaceful, less-hurried lifestyle.

We especially loved our new property and the quiet cove where it was located; there was even the added bonus of a creek running through the acreage. We initially talked about the fact that it was a good investment and how we would take vacations there; we knew in our hearts it would eventually be home. This time, though, we planned to kick back and enjoy our growing family. The leaves in the Cove were a canvas of muted colors now. Halloween had just passed, and with each new November day, more leaves were dropping. It was our first trip away from home with the new baby. Sure, there was extra to pack, but my joy of anticipating the change of scenery and promise of relaxation gave me added energy.

Bill's passion for the outdoors and wide-open spaces was fueled by the years he had invested becoming an Eagle Scout and member of the Order of the Arrow. To say he was excited about this trip seemed to be an understatement. Will easily caught his father's enthusiasm for this special holiday weekend and seemed to be filled with extra energy, too. He was enjoying the fact that he was having a lot more time with Daddy, now that baby Julie had arrived, and being Daddy's buddy was expanding his world.

We had one final stop to make before leaving. Some friends had invited us to bring Will, dressed in an animal costume, to the Noah's Ark reenactment at their church. It was an amazing event for families. The huge Noah's Ark took up the whole side of their gymnasium. The story time was fun filled with actors, puppets, and sound effects as it enraptured the audience of children, who were all dressed like animals. It was a short afternoon of fun time with friends before we settled in for the six-hour drive to the mountains.

As I reflect on that Noah's Ark party, I remember that Will was very impressed with the phrase "God shut the door!" He would say it repeatedly, especially when we would get in and out of the car that weekend. He had a unique way about repeating things. Phrases seemed to go over and over in his mind. He was very good at memorizing, and we were working on his memory verse for next Sunday, which was Ephesians 4:32, "*Be kind to one another, tenderhearted, forgiving one another"* (NIV).

He loved the four syllables of "ten-der-heart-ed" and said each syllable of the big word with a clipped, distinct rhythm. Will was a great traveler and Julie seemed to be, as well. Bill and I laughingly quipped that they had gypsy blood. We arrived on the mountain after dark, so we easily slipped our sleeping cherubs into their carefully prepared beds in the camper and woke up the next morning to a breathtaking view of Humpback Mountain.

It was idyllic, except for the occasional whistle blast of the freight trains coming around the Clinchfield Loop, jolting us into the reality of the railroad crossing that marked the entrance to our property just one hundred yards away. However, listening to sounds of the birds chirping and the nearby creek trickling over the rocks was delightful and a welcome respite. The freshness of the air was intoxicating as we hiked the country roads and the railroad tracks. We filled the next couple of days with drives along the winding mountain roads up into little country villages like Jonas Ridge and Crossnore, up toward Grandfather Mountain and Linville Falls.

Our four-day mini-vacation flew by. On our walks, we talked and planned for the days ahead. We needed to return to New Jersey to be with family for the fast-approaching holidays. When could we get away? Thanksgiving? Christmas? It was really the only time we were able to see the family anymore. The fourteen-hour trip home to Jersey was losing its appeal more and more every year we lived in the South. Will was almost four. What kind of birthday party would we have for him? My, it was coming fast; was it just four weeks away? Julie had just turned three-months old, and the family picture appointment was on the calendar for next week in plenty of time before I would send a photo card and update for the holidays. Before we would know what happened, Christmas would be here! Occupying our thoughts and conversation were the events around which most young families plan their lives and schedules.

It was such a relaxing time for us. We used this time in the mountains to discuss spiritual things, too, such as our time and focus on the church and what we sensed God was saying about our music ministry. We were determined to raise our children the way we believed God intended. We talked about our need to spend more quality time with each other and with God and what that would look like. Also, now that the baby was here, we were thinking about our evangelistic music ministry more. I had a willing heart, but I voiced concerns about my lack of energy for the present.

We agreed that we both felt God was doing something new with us. It was a time full of new beginnings and hope for brighter days ahead. Bill's life and vocation revolved around music, but there seemed to be more that he was seeking. He was searching for God's ministry purpose in his life. After delivering Julie, I felt fulfilled, and I loved my full-time role of Mommy. We both believed God was using our struggles to make us better and trusted Him to bring about a renewal of our mission as a family and to the family of God. This was reconfirmed before God as we held each other and prayed in the middle of the woods.

Dear Lord,
Please renew a right spirit in us as
we present our lives to You in service for You.
Please lead us and guide us as we trust in Your
plan for our family.

The untouched loveliness of the forest filled our souls and seemed to give us a direct connection to the One who had created all this beauty surrounding us. Will ran around us as we talked and prayed, while Julie slept peacefully in her Snuggly on my chest. He explored and picked up sticks that suited his purpose for the moment -- a mighty sword, a cowboy's gun, or a tool to practice writing his name in the dirt. The pockets of his Oshkosh overalls bulged with prized rocks and fool's gold, as well as with special leaves and precious gems.

Occasionally, we would hear Will singing or he would come and peek at the baby and practice his verse on her. "Be kind to one another tenderhearted, forgiving one another." He said it in his rhythmic clipped speech, and then he would plant what he called a *purp*, which was a loud, wet kiss her on her head.

The days had slipped away, and now it was time to close up the camper, pack up, and head back home to Charleston. The light of day was fading into night. As was our habit, we planned to travel while the children slept comfortably in their pajamas, simply to be tucked into their beds upon arrival home.

I straightened up the camper and packed our belongings. Will was outside running his matchbox cars and trucks in the track he and Daddy had made in the dirt when Bill poked his head in the door and said, "I'll be right back. I'm just going to hang this last *No Hunting* sign."

"No problem," I said. "As soon as I change the baby, I'll call Will in to get cleaned up."

A few minutes later I called Will, but he didn't answer. I went outside and looked where he had been playing. No Will. I started calling his name. When there was no response, I thought maybe he had gone with Daddy to hang the sign. Just then, I saw Bill coming through the woods with the satisfied smile of a job now completed. Will was not with him. It was then that I panicked. "Will's gone!" Hearing the panic in my voice and seeing the fear on my face, Bill immediately grabbed the flashlights by the door of the camper.

The sun was going behind the mountain quickly now; he thrust a flashlight into my hand and loudly said, "I'll go back this way. You go down the road."

I screamed with panic, "Will! Will! Where are you? Answer Mommy!" The fear and desperation in my voice and my heart were mounting.

I left the sleeping baby in her carrier in the camper and headed quickly down the mountain road toward the railroad tracks. Bill's voice carried better than mine. *Would Will even hear me? It is getting chilly. What if we can't find him?* My mind was racing with all my worst fears. *Animals were in these woods. The temperature is falling with the sun. He'll be out here in the dark and cold. He will be scared. Oh, God, please! Please.*

"Will! Will! Answer Mommy!" The minutes dragged by. *Where was he?*

"Will! Will!" I just kept moving down toward the railroad tracks, only stopping intermittently to listen for him.

Then as the train crossing came into sight, I saw our little boy running down from the knoll next to the railroad crossing at breakneck speed. He was running straight toward me and threw himself into my arms! He kept saying over and over, "I just went to find Daddy; I just went to find Daddy."

I held him tightly as I screamed to Bill, "I found him! I have him!" I couldn't put him down, even though he was far too heavy and too big to be carried. I saw Bill's flashlight beam heading toward us, but I could not release Will from my arms. Bill finally got to us and enveloped us both into his arms. We just stood there shaking with relief, trying to calm our frazzled nerves and fears, refusing to let him go until we felt calm again. I remember saying over and over, "What would we do if we ever lost you? Don't ever go away without telling Mommy or Daddy again!" Time stood still with us in those moments of relief and gratitude. We thanked God over and over for His grace, His mercy, His protection, and His goodness. We thanked God for our beloved, adventurous Will and for our beautiful family.

It was dark as we walked back together toward the camper. Julie was just waking up, but I did not want to nurse her until I was settled comfortably into the car. Bill started to load the car as I moved quickly to give Will a quick cat wash and help him into his pale blue snowman footie pajamas from Granma last Christmas. I hugged him tight again, and told him, "I love you. When you wake up, we'll be home." I gave him a kiss and a *purp*. Then, Bill carried him to the car, so his footie pajamas would stay clean and buckled him securely in his booster seat on the front passenger side of the car. In 1986, airbags were not standard. It was not uncommon for children to ride in the front seat if they were in an approved car seat.

"I wish I could just make a bed on the floor here in the back seat," I implored.

Bill responded, "No! We must obey the seat belt law. Don't worry. You know he can sleep anywhere."

I knew that was true; I just wished he could have snuggled down to sleep on soft blankets behind the front seat. Julie was fussing by now, so I got into the back seat behind Will to nurse her as Bill finished locking the camper. At least it was comfortable to nurse in the car. My lower back and shoulders had really missed my rocker at home. I was rather irritated about the handle on the bucket infant carrier, too. I could not get the handle to lower without having to twist, and that seemed to cause even more pain to my lower back. Leaving it up, I finally gave up wrestling with the handle and settled into the back seat next to the infant carrier.

We waited on Bill, while he gave final attention to securing the camper; I nursed Julie and listened as Will proudly recited his memory verse several more times. I relaxed, discounting the past hour and began to reflect at how refreshing this long weekend had been. Wow! We made it through baby's first camping trip. Nursing made it easy -- no bottles to fuss with. The milk was always the right temperature, but that stubborn carrier handle and nursing was taking its toll on my back. Now, it was time to sit back and rest. Bill loved to drive, and the seven hours would go by quickly. I was eagerly anticipating getting back home to resume our routine and to comfortably sleep in our bed and rock in my rocking chair. As I settled back in the seat, I was most grateful for our family and the reconnecting of our souls with each other and with God. All things being counted, it had been a wonderful trip.

III

God's Protection

*"For we do not wrestle flesh and blood, but against principal-
ities, against powers, against the rulers of the darkness of this
age, and against spiritual hosts of wickedness in the heavenly
places."*

Ephesians 6:12 (NKJV)

In the darkness of the night, the crackling sound of Bill's
candy bar wrapper woke me. I hadn't intended to doze off. Will
and Julie were still sound asleep: Will was in his car seat on the
front passenger side, and Julie was in her rear-facing infant seat in
the center back with me. We preferred traveling at night because
there were usually fewer cars on the road, and the children were
able to sleep peacefully. Bill, whose eyes usually felt the strain of
reading books, never minded night driving; in fact, he especially
liked to use his time behind the wheel to listen to books on tape.
On this particular trip, he was listening to a Christian parenting
tape series. I shivered from the brisk air blowing through Bill's
partially opened window. I reached around to the front passenger
seat and adjusted the pillow, cradling Will's head. He stirred a
little, but a reassuring pat from his dad was all he needed to settle
back down. It was 1:30 a.m. November 5, 1986.

I felt there was too much air blowing over the baby, so I
took Bill's flannel jacket lying nearby on the back seat and draped
it over the upright handle of the infant seat. That handle! I had

borrowed a bucket baby car seat for this trip from my sweet neighbor, Ginny. While it made the car seat easy to grab while getting in and out of the car with the baby, the handle on it had been a source of irritation for me throughout the whole trip. I had to be a contortionist to adjust the handle down, once inside the car. *Now,* I thought to myself, *that handle staying up will finally serve a purpose!* I draped the handle with Bill's jacket, and it was immediately transformed into a windbreaker, totally blocking the breeze and making a snug cocoon for the baby. Perfect!

Bill glanced back at me and said, "I'm going to stop for gas at the next exit, so we should get out and stretch. We're almost in Columbia." Then, with a smile and a wink, he softly exclaimed, "Halfway home!"

The chill of this early November night caused me to shiver, but inside I was warm, peaceful, and content. It had been a relaxing, restorative trip; I was living my dream. I had everything I had always wanted in this car: two beautiful, healthy children and a man who loved me and who wanted to serve God. This was my family. I felt so full and beyond blessed. I wrapped my sweater a little tighter around me and settled back in the seat.

In the surrounding blackness of the night with only the sounds of the road and the hypnotic rhythm of the tires, I felt peacefully encased with the loves of my life. Then, in the next moment -- a deafening explosion! An overwhelming noise! A startling invasion! An intrusion of something huge and hideous with no defined shape. Sounds of glass shattering -- metal crunching -- wind ripping -- cloth tearing – blackness – evil! Death swept through our car! 'It couldn't get out. We all were in its way! *Oh, God, oh God! What is it?* Terrifying noises and gripping fear created on the sound stage of a horror movie would be the only way to describe the terror – blackness – death -- of what I heard and felt at this moment.

We had been traveling on I-26 in our Chrysler LeBaron at about sixty-five miles per hour most of the way. But Bill had slowed down a little in preparation for the gas exit coming up soon. We had driven under an overpass. Bill was frantically trying to control the car as he threw it into park and pulled the emergency brake up to slow us down. While desperately trying to steer the car to the side of the road, he managed to open his door and drag his left leg on the highway, trying to stop the car and get it over to the side of the road. As the car came to a halt, we quickly moved into assessment mode.

Bill had lost his glasses in the explosive impact. He could barely see on the dark highway in the blackness of the night. He immediately reached for the CB radio to call for help. He didn't want to waste a moment, so he did not wait for an answer.

The baby was wailing and screaming. Even though she was seated right next to me, I couldn't get to her because she was totally covered up by something dark, massive, and very heavy. When I quickly took a look over the front seat at Will, he looked like he was sleeping peacefully. My mind raced! *How could he have slept through all of this noise? I can't get to the baby! The screaming! She's injured! What happened? I can't get the car door to open! Did we hit something?*

Bill was out of the car and frantic to get the passenger door open to check on Will. He needed to grab an extra pair of glasses out of the glove box. I kicked at the front passenger door from the back seat, and after a few tries, it came free.

Bill said, "Get the baby! I've got Will."

I yelled to him that I couldn't get to her. Whatever the

massive intruder was, I couldn't move it off her. Bill ran around to the rear driver's side door. I was frantically trying to push the object off her, but it would not budge.

Bill reached over the *mass* and said, "As I pull, you push up."

Working together, we rolled a massive rock off the baby carrier. Much later, we would learn that it was a granite boulder weighing 189 pounds that had come to rest on top of our three-month-old daughter, who weighed eleven pounds, in her infant carrier.

I quickly unbuckled and scooped Julie out of the infant seat and scrambled out of the back seat of the car. Frantic to calm my screaming, hysterical baby, I pulled up my shirt and nursed her standing at the side of the highway, holding, rocking, and desperately trying to calm her until we could assess her injuries. Bill rushed back to Will's side. He also tried to flag down cars, but none stopped. He tried the CB again, this time hearing from a trucker, but the connection kept breaking up.

Before we even had a moment to speak to each other, a car pulled over, coming to a stop behind us. A man immediately came over to the passenger side of the car where I was standing, trying to calm the baby and to stay near our son, too. I realized Will was unconscious at that point and still buckled in his car seat. I just knew we had to get him to a hospital. He needed help! We needed help! The *Good Samaritan* spoke very calmly as he assessed the situation and asked me to get a blanket.

He said, "We need to keep him warm; help is on its way."

In the darkness by the side of the road with only the dim overhead light of the car, I handed Bill the baby as I scrambled to grab a blanket from the back seat. The man stepped aside so that I could tuck it around Will. I saw a triangle-shaped wound at Will's temple and realized that he would need medical attention right away.

I saw that Will's little *blankie* had slipped out of his hand next to his booster seat. He was growing up; he only used his *blankie* to settle down for sleep these days. This corner piece of the blanket was the one with the original *spot*, a hole he had worked into the satin binding corner for his index finger to slip into and hold the blanket as he sucked his thumb. I had previously cut his favorite blanket into four squares, each with a corner piece, so he would always have a clean *spot* to suck his thumb when he was going to sleep.

I scooped it up and jammed it into the pocket of my jeans thinking he would need it later at the hospital. I was already anticipating the future in my head and begging God, *oh, please God . . . please don't let him be hurt too badly! If I must push him in a wheelchair, I'll take care of him. I'll do whatever it takes, just don't take him . . . no matter what . . . please Lord, please help him*! At that moment I heard the siren of an ambulance coming. *The truckers must have heard our SOS! Thank you, God!* Someone had called an ambulance!

The ambulance pulled over behind the other car, and it was only then that I realized that Bill was limping and bloody. I was also bleeding from head wounds. Nothing mattered except they get to Will ASAP! Bill and the man were talking to one of the medics. Another one of the EMS workers took the whimpering baby from me, and I followed him because I felt I needed to stay with her. Someone had gotten the baby carrier out of the car, and they were asking me to get into the ambulance, so they could take us to the hospital. I numbly complied and sat down for a moment.

Then, in one split moment, it hit me that we were leaving

without Will. We were about to leave Will behind! *No! No! No!*
The one place where I could not allow my thoughts to go forced
itself on me! My worst fear! *"NO!"*

I bolted out of the ambulance, leaving the baby behind
with a startled EMS worker and ran to Will, still strapped into
his car seat. I looked at Bill standing by the car. One look at
the anguish on his face confirmed the deepest, blackest horror
of my soul. I could feel myself going numb, slipping away . . .
somewhere far away . . . a place I didn't want to go . . . dark . . .
ugly . . . cold . . . dreadful . . . hideous . . . inertia was setting in
and forcing me down into an abyss where there seemed to be no
bottom. There was a paralyzing force that assaulted my mind and
stifled my breath. *No! No! No!*

I wanted to scream! I wanted to wake up! I wanted to be
home! But instead of falling into the abyss, I turned toward a
pinpoint of light, running into a small, dark room somewhere
deep within my soul. It was a safe place; no one could hear me
screaming there, and no one could find me. In that dimly lit room
in my head, I was a young girl about seven years old and dressed in
a blue shirtwaist dress. I stood all alone but felt safe and strangely
comforted by a small beam of light coming through a high, tiny
window. This place, deep inside my soul, was my place to escape. I
wanted to stay and scream some more inside that room. Instead, I
numbly looked at my busy, bright, funny, perfect little boy, lifeless
in his car seat, dressed warmly in his snowman pajamas.

We knelt by the highway that night, Bill and me, crying
out to our Creator in horror and disbelief that this had even
happened. In our anguish and our pain, we simply turned to
God for comfort and help. He would have to carry us now in the
same way we had picked up and carried our precious children.

He would care for us. We had to believe and trust that HE would make sense of this. The foundation of our faith was John 3:16: *"God,"* the perfect Father, *"so loved the world that He gave His only begotten Son, so that whoever believes on Him would have eternal life."*

Next to Will's lifeless body, I held tightly to my husband's big hand as he placed his other one on Will's head. Bill began to pray out loud, "Thank you, Lord, for giving us our son Will to love and care for. We don't understand You Heavenly Father, but we trust You. You gave us a most precious gift to love, and we release and give his sweet spirit back to you. Amen."

It was a simple prayer during one moment in time, which is engraved on my heart and kept forever in my treasure box of memories. Even as I write this, my mind takes me straight back to the day when Will was born, when DeEtte, our midwife, moved aside as she spoke to Bill, "Go ahead! Catch your baby!"

And Bill, grinning from ear to ear, said to me, "Here he is Lin . . . . God's Will!"

I still marvel at Bill's presence of mind during this time when I felt so weak, so numb, and so helpless. On the side of I-26, I kissed Will's beautiful face that night, caressed his sweet, soft creamy skin, and tousled his hair the same way I did every night as I tucked him into bed. This night, I clung onto his lifeless little body, still buckled in his booster seat. I did not want to let him go. I wanted to hold him and rock him. I wanted to tell him he would be OK and that the doctors would make him better. I did not want to leave him behind with strangers, well-meaning strangers or not!

Why can't I take him out of the car seat? I screamed inside my head. I felt like we were abandoning him! I felt so helpless not being able to stay with him. I don't believe I ever spoke the question out loud, but whether I did or not, Bill said understandingly, "The police say we can't move him."

Now, more than ever, we needed to believe in a plan bigger than us. A plan that would help draw us closer to God. We had to believe because we needed Him so desperately. I don't know exactly what we prayed, but I do know that we knelt and prayed on that dark highway that horrible night. We prayed in a language that we didn't understand but one that comes through the Holy Spirit that only God can give. In and of ourselves, we had no strength; we didn't know how to pray or even what to pray. I do know that kneeling by the side of Hwy I-26 that night and praying beyond our understanding connected us directly to our Creator -- our Heavenly Father -- our God, in a way that brought us peace beyond our understanding and gave us supernatural strength for the moments, hours, and days ahead.

He came down to us that night through His Holy Spirit. He was with us. He brought us a comfort and deep peace that I still do not understand. We didn't know what else to do. We had no control, no say. We were overwhelmingly helpless to do anything but trust in a God we did not understand. There were no words spoken in the ambulance as we headed to the hospital -- only somber silence. After praying beside the highway that night, a scripture that I had never intentionally memorized began to loop through my mind. *"We wrestle not against flesh and blood but against principalities of the air."* I kept saying it under my breath; it was like a puzzle piece in my hand. I didn't know exactly where it belonged, but deep in my heart, I knew that it was a piece of the puzzle for what lay ahead.

IV

God's Proclamation

". . . My strength is made perfect in your weakness . . . . For when I am weak then I am strong."

2 Corinthians 12: 9-10 (NKJV)

The news of the tragedy and anguish of our souls had preceded our arrival to the hospital. The mood was somber as we entered the Lexington County Hospital and were led down an unoccupied hallway. The hospital was eerily silent and seemed almost empty. They were obviously prepared for our arrival as we were escorted to an area that had been cordoned off for us. I did not even see or hear another patient that night. Bill was swiftly whisked away to X-ray for his leg injuries. A nurse appeared and talked softly to me about the baby. She explained that they needed to get her x-rayed immediately. Julie weighed eleven pounds at 3 ½ months old, still tiny for her age. She had cuts and scrapes on her soft infant head.

Please dear God, please let her be OK, I kept praying under my breath. Not allowing any thoughts to go back to the highway, I coped by focusing on the baby instead of thinking about the wrenching horror of leaving Will behind. I stayed with the baby as the nurse strapped her down to be x-rayed. She whimpered but seemed to be exhausted from all her crying. I only moved away from her when the actual pictures were taken.

I then followed the nurse to the curtain-draped cubicle. The gentle nurse treated Julie's cuts and scrapes as I continued to hold on to my precious bundle. After we had done a thorough assessment of the baby's injuries, she turned to me. Up until that time, I had not even felt my wounds, but after her tender yet thorough cleansing of my contusions and abrasions and scrapes on my head, I became more aware of the pain sustained from the object that hit me and from the pelting shards of shattered glass. She carefully undid my waist-long French-braided hair and proceeded to methodically brush, from the ends up toward the scalp. She combed out the shards of glass and treated my cuts and abrasions. This was no small task as she ministered to my needs; there was minimal chatting. I was numb, caught up in the black horror and anguish of my loss.

I can still remember the sweet, sad expression in her eyes and her gentle touch that needed no words to express her grief. "Can I get you something or do anything else for you?" She asked softly. "I can bring in a little bed for the baby." I shook my head from side to side and mouthed a "No thank you" and continued to hold the baby who, by now, was exhausted and peacefully asleep. The nurse left me, and I settled back into the chair to wait for Bill.

I closed my eyes, deflated in spirit and in hopeless despair. What appeared before me in the next moment was something that would be forever burned into my mind. As long as I breathe, I will never forget what I saw. It was real and vibrantly alive! It was a living picture of two men, standing side by side. They were up high above me and standing together. The tallest was over ten feet tall. He was completely clothed in a long white robe, and His face was brilliantly shining, beautiful and peaceful. His expression was very serious and somber. In my mind, I identified the face as that of Jesus Christ. The brilliant light on it had the bright ambiguous definition of an over-exposed photo, while the light emanating from Him was clear and pure. His arms were covered by the fullness of the long sleeve of the flowing robe, exposing His hands that were outstretched as though they were in a position to pick up or catch something. I saw the scars on His open hands. I knew I was seeing my Jesus. He was standing very close to another man who was considerably shorter.

The top of the shorter man's head barely reached the other man's shoulders. They were standing beside each other, so close that a piece of paper couldn't have been slid between them. The shorter man, handsome and blonde, was dressed in an ominous black full-length robe with long voluminous sleeves. I knew I was looking straight into the face of Satan! He was cradling a huge rock in his arms, as though he were holding a baby. At the bottom hem of both men's robes was a low white fence.

As I numbly stared at the living picture, I heard a clear strong voice that spoke: "My Daughter, I AM BIGGER."

In my mind I thought, *Yes! Wow! I can see that,* and then the voice said, "REMEMBER JOB!"

Bill's voice broke into the moment, and the *living picture* instantly disappeared. Bill was being rolled out of X-ray on a stretcher and being placed in a cubicle across from me. He called to me through the curtain, "Lin? Are you there?"

"Yes," I answered weakly.

Bill said, "We must remember Job, Lin. We must remember Job."

Chill bumps flooded my soul and covered my arms. I sadly replied, "I know."

Comforted, yet awed by the *living picture* and hearing *The Voice* brought a sense of peace and stability to the wonder and bewilderment. Some things are just true whether one believes in them or not. I believe God gave me just what I needed to make it through this time. Even in my despair, HIS comfort was felt and treasured. It also gave me the faith and confidence I needed to know that God was right here with us and that He really was *BIGGER*. HE had just visually illustrated that! I would choose to believe and trust in a God who was BIGGER than this tragedy, this pain, this devastation. I believed with all my being that we weren't wrestling with the natural (the flesh and blood); we were in the middle of a Spiritual battle! It seemed to help make sense of the scripture verse scrolling through my thoughts like a weather alert, running across the bottom of the television screen. The verse about "not wrestling flesh and blood, but principalities of the air" occupied my mind.

You may have trouble grasping what I am recalling, but I am certain that I was far too fractured emotionally to imagine anything so wonderful! It was the beauty of who God is to give us just what we need when we need it. This *living picture's* deeper meaning would continue to unfold in the months ahead.

I knew very little at the time about JOB. I had been raised in a home, which meant Sunday school every Sunday and lots of Bible stories, but *the patience of JOB* was the only expression I could remember concerning the book of JOB. For now, in the hospital, I decided I would have to research that at another time. What was the meaning of all this? I only wanted to turn back the clock of time. Maybe I would awaken from this hellish nightmare.

Even as I write, the words of the great Christian author, C.S. Lewis, ring so true. "God speaks to us in our conscience, shouts to us in our pain, but whispers to us in our pleasures." God seemed to be shouting to us in our pain. He was right there with us. I wasn't even trying to trust Him. Even though I had visited Heaven, all I really wanted was a do over. This was a horrible nightmare! I wanted to hold my little boy. I wanted to be planning his fourth birthday party just a few weeks away. I wanted him back! God certainly seemed to be shouting to us through this heartache.

Our friends, Phil and Barbara, from Charleston arrived and were ushered into the eerily quiet hospital area they had made for us. They hugged us and cried with us, and then they said that one of the things God had been telling them was to "remember JOB." One more confirmation from God! Our parents and families lived so far away, so an added measure of calm and support came with the arrival of Philip and Barbara.

They were friends from our church who had become like life coaches, especially in the area of our marriage relationship. Just their presence comforted Bill and me. I remember telling Barbara and Phil of how we thought we had lost Will in the woods and how God had gifted us with that special time of affirmation and love. Talking about our wonderful time in the mountains helped to hold back the flood gates of tears and raw emotions.

Bill and I were as fractured as the windshield of our car, desperately trying to hold the remnants of our lives together. There were few words spoken between Bill and me; we had both been "sucker punched." The wind had been knocked out of us. We couldn't even help each other. Just having our friends sitting quietly nearby with their lips moving in silent sacred prayer helped us.

Through the dark hours at the hospital, we were in contact

with the police while our injuries were being treated. The Good Samaritan to arrive first on the interstate had turned out to be an off-duty detective named P.C.Faglie. He would become the investigator in charge and our constant contact with the police department. Detective Faglie had just gotten off duty and was heading home on I-26 when he heard the emergency call on the CB. He saw us on the other side of the highway and took the next exit. It had seemed as though he were there almost immediately. Over the years, I have often reflected on the timing of the appearance of P.C. He seemed heaven sent, or at the very least, God had scheduled an appointment for him that night, and he had responded without reservation.

We kept asking whether Will's body had been brought to the hospital yet. For a couple of hours no one seemed to know. This was also when we found out that the huge granite rock that came out of nowhere did not come loose from a mountain but had been intentionally placed and dropped off the overpass as we traveled underneath. We learned that this had been a deliberate, calculated, and malicious act of violence!

When the word came through the police that Will's body had arrived at the hospital, we insisted that we be with him. We only wanted to hold him, to rock him, to touch him one more time. Hospital policy, however, said no -- another blow to the heart! On top of the entire trauma now, once again, we were refused the simple request to be with our dead son's body! Would this nightmare never end? Bill fully believed that God would resurrect Will, and he grew increasingly frustrated as we were denied access to him. I didn't even know what to pray except, *Please LORD give him back. I only want him back! Please God!* My God had raised His own son from the dead. Surely, he *could* do it, but *would* He? We just wanted to hold him; to be with him. He had been cruelly ripped from our arms. It seemed so unfathomable to not let us even cradle him in our grief.

In his state of mind, Bill angrily tried to barge through some doors to find him. The nurses summoned orderlies to restrain him. What parent wouldn't want to be with his child? Apparently, Bill was thinking along the same line, as he dejectedly asked, "Is there a chapel in the hospital where we could go?"

The nurse answered, "Yes. I'll take you". Forcing us to surrender to a senseless and cruel hospital policy seemed so heartless.

Today, most hospitals have a Patients' Bill of Rights, but that was not until 1992. Meantime, Bill convinced another compassionate nurse to take my compact mirror into the morgue and place it at Will's nose and mouth to reassure us that he had not breathed for at least fifteen minutes. The nurse and a doctor honored Bill's request by doing that for us while we prayed in the chapel.

We headed to the chapel with the baby and our friends, including Pastor Green, a friend of Barbara and Phil's, who had just arrived at the hospital. He quietly led us in prayer, and the presence of the Lord filled the room as we united our hearts in faith and prayed fervently for Will's life to be restored. Bill laid face down on the floor of the chapel altar and begged and pleaded with God to bring Will's life back into his body. Bill's crying and wailing was overwhelming to me. I couldn't comfort him; I couldn't comfort myself. I couldn't join him in his grief. I felt that if I gave in, I would do a freefall into a dark, bottomless abyss and never return. I felt frozen and unable to move. Bill, though, was offering his life for his son's life, as Barbara would later write about her memories of that night.

When I thought about the Lord in the Garden of Gethsemane, I only thought about the agony Jesus suffered. But now I see it from a different viewpoint. In the Garden Experience with Bill, I watched a father in agony over the loss of his only son, exceedingly sorrowful, weeping at the altar, hurting beyond words, yet enduring the best he could. He encouraged himself by quoting scriptures and by reaching out for strength, yet he was aching inside to hold his only son whom he dearly loved. And I realized while Jesus was suffering in agony, God was suffering, as well. It would have been easier for God to have given Himself than to give us His Son.

My heart ached for us all to be together. I wanted to hold Will, to comfort him. Was he looking for us in that big, beautiful place in the sky? Probably not, I reasoned in my head. I had been so enveloped in my Heavenly experience that even I hadn't wanted to come home from my trip there. Will was running on ahead, as usual. But he had always had Mommy or Daddy with him! Why God? Why?

We were all physically wounded, but the mortal wounding of my soul would require healing that was not available at the hospital. I could barely function. To this day, I don't know why I couldn't plead for Will's life with Bill. Maybe I didn't have enough faith that God would return life to him, or maybe I was beginning to let God be BIGGER. Then again, maybe I was just shutting down. Content to be in that dark little room with the pinpoint of light above me. This was not over, and no matter what, I continued to hold tightly to Julie, feeling like a scared little girl with her baby doll.

It was no longer dark; the sun was rising on a new day.

It was not until dawn that I would make the phone call to my parents in New Jersey. In 1986, a cell phone in every hand was near, yet still in the future. As a nurse dialed my parents' phone number, I was feeling intense exhaustion at this point in time. I was just going through the motions. All of this seemed unreal. I wanted it not to be true. I was devastated. The words coming out of my mouth did not even seem to belong to me.

My father answered the phone, as I pictured my mother heading for the extension, "Daddy . . . this is Linda. . . ."

I would begin to cry and relive the horror all over again as I relayed the circumstances to them. I sobbed when I told my parents that Will was dead. Bill took over the phone call. Even with their own shock and anguish, my parents volunteered to go over to see Bill's parents personally and tell them of the tragedy. They promised us that they would get on the next flight to Charleston and come as quickly as they could. My father prayed with us before they hung up and assured us of their love and prayers. We were being released from the hospital. *How can we go home to Charleston without our son? He was ours -- God had placed him in my womb -- He made me a mom -- we can't just walk away -- Where was our car?* Columbia had just been a gas and rest stop for us. We knew nothing of the area. *What now? What happens next? Can we have our child back? Where is our little boy?* I was silently screaming again at the top of my lungs standing with clenched fists in the small dark room inside my head!

The police secured a room for us at the Ramada Inn across from the hospital, so we could shower and change. Our car was at the impound lot. We would have to get some things from our car. The suggestion was that we might try and get a little sleep. At this point, we had been awake for more than twenty-four hours. The coroner was not going to release Will's body without an autopsy because they were calling this crime a homicide. A murder? What did all this mean? Someone did this on purpose? By now, all we really had learned through the night was that a huge boulder came out of nowhere and irreparably ripped through our lives. We were shattered! We had just come from the mountains where rockslides are somewhat familiar, and it seemed logical and far more realistic to think that maybe that was what had happened. We had received no warnings or premonitions to let us know of the danger that was ahead of us. I had no idea how we would get through this, but of one thing I was certain -- HE was BIGGER than all of this! Somewhere deep inside, I believed it, and it became my anchor!

Phillip and Barbara accompanied us as we left the hospital in Columbia and checked into a hotel room for some rest and showers. Phillip took Bill to the impound lot to get a suitcase with a change of clothes for us since ours were bloody and torn. They also transferred other items from our car. The plan was to have our friends drive us home to Charleston but not until Will's body was released from the coroner. I left the napping baby with Barbara and Phillip. Bill and I entered the hotel room. For the first time since all this happened, Bill and I were alone. Once we faced each other, and I looked into Bill's eyes, we fell into a freefall of gut-wrenching despair and sorrow as we sobbed and clung to each other in shared grief until exhausted and depleted. We were too exhausted to continue crying. We showered and changed into clean clothes, but no real rest or refreshment came. We just waited for the hotel room phone to ring from the coroner's office.

Officer P.C. Faglie was a constant source of help and support for us. The calm, assuring presence of the man who told me to keep Will warm continued doing his sworn duty with an amazing presence of mind and tender heart. We learned from him that they believed that two teenage boys had done this and that the police had already been looking for the boys because they had missed a probation appointment and had stolen a moped the previous day. The police had dogs out during the night, and they had successfully apprehended both within an hour of the incident. Both boys were now in police custody. *What now? Where do we go from here?* We had a child to bury. We had to have a funeral.

V

God's Presence

"Now the one who has fashioned us for this very purpose is God, who has given us the Spirit as a deposit, guaranteeing what is to come. Therefore, we are always confident and know that as long as we are at home in the body we are away from the Lord. For we live by faith, not by sight. We are confident, I say, and would prefer to be away from the body and at home with the Lord."

— 2 Corinthians 5: 5-8 (NIV)

How do you have a funeral for a child? Mom and Dad were coming. *I can't do this, but they can,* I thought. I needed them! I retreated further into my own thoughts. In my mind, I was still a small young girl. I was standing all alone, frightened beyond words. I stood in that tiny dark room with the one tiny ray of light. Every time my thoughts got too overwhelming, I would run to that place and scream as loud and as long as I wanted to. It was a safe place where no one could hear me or stop me, and I would scream loud so that I could not hear anything else. I would make many trips to that small dark room in the days ahead.

A couple of hours later, the call finally came in from the coroner. They were releasing Will's body to the Funeral Chapel in Charleston. Bill and Phil had transferred our retrieved belongings and filled the trunk of their car. We left behind our impounded car, which now had become evidence in the murder. Sadly, the memory of this horrific night would become a permanent piece of the fabric of the battered remnant of our young family. The final miles of our *mini vacation* had now turned into a funeral procession as we followed the *hearse* home that carried the precious body of our little Will. We still had not seen or touched him since we prayed over him and left him buckled in his booster chair in our car on I-26. Now, we simply had to trust that it was his body in a van directly in front of us, heading to a funeral home. He should have been heading home to his comfy blue race car bed! My head was pounding. The horror of the night was crushing in again. I ran once again to my small dark room.

We followed the van down I-26 until we had to take the exit to our home. As the van continued its way to Charleston, carrying its precious cargo, I could feel my heart beginning to race. I got clammy and anxious. I could barely breathe. The closer we got to our home, I knew I wasn't ready to go back to our house without him -- our little home with memories of the sound of Will running down the hall, playing and laughing. I knew I'd see Will's toys scattered about, Will's bed, Will's things. Everything would be familiar except I wouldn't hear him, I wouldn't see him, I couldn't hold him, I would never get to hug and kiss him goodnight again. I couldn't do this! I didn't want to live without him! I couldn't breathe, and I started to run toward my dark room.

Barbara and Phil were already expecting my parents would be staying at their home since our home was small. I was relieved when Barbara and Phil thought it best that we stay with them as well. We went straight to their home as they graciously opened their lives and hearts to us. Our tragedy took over their quiet, unassuming lives when they willingly gave us all they could give. They served us with an amazing love and sacrifice. They embraced us as their own. How would I ever repay their generosity? It would just be the beginning of a long thank you list that I would keep in my heart but never be able to address.

Friends and family were in and out through the days that followed. I hurt so badly. That first night when Bill and I were alone, he looked at me with deep anguish in his eyes and said flatly, "You know, it's your fault." It wasn't an accusation as much as it was a statement of fact. I knew immediately what he was saying. I had already been blaming myself.

I had already lived my whole life as the over-responsible first-born child. I was an expert at self-condemnation. Somehow, even growing up as the oldest of five children, whenever anything went wrong, there would be some way that I always felt it was my fault. As the oldest, I had been expected to set the right example -- to do the right thing no matter what the cost. It was a deep-seated pattern that I had carried into my marriage. I had figured out long ago that taking the blame and doing what needed to be done was easier than dealing with the conflict. I had been raised in a home where peace at any price was normal and the blame game was continually played. After all, men have been blaming women since Adam blamed God for giving him Eve in the garden, so I thought it was just how it was.

I knew Bill was referring to "our sin." It was the sin that we had promised one another years ago that we would take to our graves. Oh, dear God! I don't know how YOU can be BIGGER than all this, I thought. I felt nothing but hopelessness as the accusing voice in my head kept whispering in overwhelming condemnation: Guilty! Guilty! Guilty! Over and over the judge's gavel hammered this into my mind. The wage of sin is death. But the voice of truth through His Word in my heart would resonate over the pounding gavel. "My gift is eternal life! You will see Will again. I showed you My special place. I promise. I AM BIGGER!"

VI

God's Peace

*"For none of us lives for ourselves alone, and none of us dies
for ourselves alone. If we live, we live for the Lord; and if we
die, we die for the Lord. So, whether we live or die, we belong
to the Lord. For this very reason, Christ died and returned to life
so that he might be the Lord of both the dead and the living."*

Romans 14:7-9 (NIV)

I continually held Julie. She was my comfort. Somehow, I
didn't feel as empty when she was in my arms. Julie was my excuse
to refuse medication when others wanted to give me medicine
to sleep. I reasoned, "I must stay alert for the baby. I want to
continue to nurse her, and she needs me to be all here for her."

Julie became both a comfort and an anchor of connection
to God and to the present for me. She was another precious
gift from HIM, and I could feel HIM through her. From the
time she was born we had called her our snuggle bunny; she just
loved being held. Holding, rocking, and nursing her forced me to
practice inner calmness as I was determined to focus my mind
and thoughts on good things so that her life would not be too
deeply affected by my heartache.

There was a deep resolve within me that did not want to
miss out on any of the circumstances in which we found ourselves.
I felt a peace beyond myself and knew HE was carrying me. I

felt my Heavenly Father's very real supernatural presence as HE endeavored to bring me a measure of comfort. I did not really understand HIS seeming cruelty at this point, but my experience in Heaven and hearing the gentleness of the messenger's voice speak my name, brought to me a supernatural comfort. Even in the agony of the present, HE was more real to me than the events of the day. I would think a lot about my trip to Heaven, longing to be there with Will. Was he playing with the other children, the ones I saw in Heaven? I knew he didn't even miss us; he was on an adventure with no concept of time, and he would never want it to end. I thought about the living picture bringing me back to the circumstances in our present, and I wondered what was happening in God's unseen bigger plan. I would ponder the vision of Jesus and Satan as I read and reread the first chapter of the book of Job. I would hear HIS strong voice saying over and over, "I AM BIGGER." It brought me great comfort to know God was speaking to me.

Bill and I wondered if we would get any restful sleep as we tried to grasp for something about this ordeal that made sense. Bill had come into the bedroom where I was with the sleeping baby, and I had my Bible open on the bed where I was desperately looking for a word of comfort. He said, "There is a verse in Proverbs that says something about sweet sleep . . . do you think you can find it?"

I found it in Chapter 3, verse 24: "*When you lie down, you will not be afraid; yes, you will lie down, and your sleep will be sweet*" (NKJV). We sat on the side of the bed, hand in hand, and in our exhaustion, simply asked God to make this verse true in our lives. True to His Word, He did! I can honestly say that we both slept soundly each night after reading that Word of Promise, and we did not even dream during that first week after Will's death. Together, and individually, we took God at His Word in a very simple, childlike way. HE was showing us we could still trust in HIM, especially in the little things. As I repeated HIS promise over and over, it would quiet my thoughts, and I would fall asleep.

My parents and church family handled most of our needs. Family and friends were only too willing to let me retreat into my head, holding tightly onto Julie. Even as Barbara and Phil's home would flood with comforters, I retreated to the bedroom and rocked the baby. Most of my prayers were filled with repentance for every wrong I had done. I found myself making deals with Him if HE would just return our son. I so wanted a Lazarus story, a resurrection. Many people worried about me, but I believe even more people prayed.

We drove to the funeral home in a rental car two days later to begin to make arrangements. I did not want to be in that place, a place I would never choose to bring a young child, yet he was already here! I was silently screaming again in my head, but no one could hear; would anyone even understand? I asked to see Will but was told again that they could not let me see him until his body was prepared. *I just want him back . . . I am his mother . . . . God made me his mother . . . . I need to see him, touch him . . . doesn't anyone understand?* Inside my mind, I was a wreck having a temper tantrum; on the outside, I complied.

Bill and I numbly worked out the details of the funeral. I carefully chose the clothes Will would wear. He wasn't a toddler anymore. He had grown up so much this year. He would wear big-boy transformer underwear and little man pants, tailored with all the pockets and front zipper with a leather belt like his dad's, along with a bold blue and red stripe, white-collared knit sport shirt and crew socks with a blue and red stripe. I had his clothes carefully folded, and I carried them to the funeral home.

It had been three days, and we still had not seen his body since that night on I-26. I think I had hoped they would let me hold him and let me help dress him one more time. Oh, how I just wanted to hold my precious little boy! I wanted to help dress him one last time! I missed him so much. I physically longed to touch him and ached all over as though I were in withdrawal. The nightmare of that black, death-filled night, as well as still not having him by my side, churned my stomach.

Bill and I separated at the funeral home. Bill went with one man to handle the cost of this horror, and I went with another man as I would have the task of picking out a container for his dear little body. I tried to focus as I was led into a room full of coffins. The sympathetic funeral director tried to explain, "Most caskets are not sized for children. We are very limited on what we can show you." Would this nightmare never end?

In the casket room was a big alcove-like display closet. Inside this large closet area were floor to ceiling shelves. Filling the shelves were babies' and children's coffins. I would find myself examining small coffins made of different thicknesses of cardboard covered with various types of white fabric. Some were plain; some had fancier stitching; and, some were covered in satin, while others were wrapped in organza. In this suffocating nightmare of shopping, my mind immediately went back to a childhood memory of placing our beloved pet parakeet *Blue Boy* into a shoebox lined with soft white tissues and ceremoniously burying it in the back yard. Even as a child I understood our bird would never return, and its body would decompose quickly.

I felt physically nauseous. I knew this was difficult for both of us. In a room full of different style coffins, they had only one coffin that would fit Will's size. It was silver/gray metal and about four feet long. Even though I hated this one, at least it wasn't a cardboard box. He was too big for the white boxes. This metal coffin would have to do. It was just another horror piled on top of all the other ones. The pale silver metal coffin seemed so cold to me -- a tin box in which to put my warm, affectionate loving little boy. All alone, I would scream hysterically, standing in the center of the dark, suffocating small room in my mind where no one could hear. I would hope that the light would grow brighter and absorb me into it as I reluctantly left the funeral home that possessed my son.

By now, all my sisters, my brother and their young families assembled in South Carolina. Deep sadness, shock, numbness . . . . Most of the family that was coming had arrived from New Jersey and Pennsylvania. Four days had dragged by. The service came together with help from our good friend Lee and Pastor Larry. Their guidance through this time was treasured.

There are no manuals written on how to have a funeral for a child, but we ultimately decided to celebrate Will's brief life, play his favorite songs, and give people an opportunity to share their thoughts and memories. Before we did that though, it was finally time for us to reunite with the lifeless body of our precious son, whose brief young life had defined us as *Mommy* and *Daddy*.

We drove to the funeral home in Charleston for a private viewing the afternoon before the funeral service, which was scheduled for the next day. I did not even know how to prepare myself. I only wanted to be near him. I hoped I could hold him, dreading the thought that I would see my little fellow in that awful coffin. I will always be grateful for the attendant who made sure I was able to go in alone, first, to see Will. It was to make sure everything was done to my instructions. I had voiced my desire to want to dress him for the last time because that's what Mommies do, but this was their compromise of helping me get him ready for *company*.

He was wearing the clothes I picked out for him. Did I mention that I couldn't find his shoes? I was only able to find his socks; much later I would realize that his *dress shoes* were still under the front seat in the car at the impound lot in Columbia. I had been the one to care for him, wash him, and dress him. I knew every inch of his perfect little body, even though I knew he was no longer in this precious *earth suit* in front of me. I had been his caregiver, and he had been entrusted to me. I rationalized to myself; *He doesn't need his shoes . . . he never really liked shoes much anyway . . . he took after me when it came to shoes. I just don't wear them unless I must, and now he doesn't have to either!* He was free now from the confines of the things of this world, and that included his shoes!

I was tenderly surprised that he looked so peaceful and asleep, except for the silent stillness. I touched him gently with my hand, and the coldness sent shivers through my soul. *Please Lord*, I sent up a quick SOS prayer; *help me! I need You!*

The way they had combed his hair and the makeup they used to cover the wound really troubled me. The perceptive attendant seemed to sense my next thought and handed me a small comb from his pocket.

"Here, Mrs. Stapleton. You fix his hair."

That gentleman will never know how much that gesture of kindness meant to me in that moment to be able to muss up Will's hair and just pat it in place as I politely refused the comb.

I took my time as I held his little hands in mine, put my cheek against his lifeless one, cradled his dear, beautiful flawless face, and placed each memory and detail into my mind's treasure box. That's all we had ever desired to do on the interstate and at the hospital. I needed to tenderly caress him, touch him, and be still and quiet with him one more time. Time stood still for me. I put his choo-choo train pillowcase on the pillow under his head and placed his right index finger into his *blankie's* worn, special spot.

As I studied the wound at Will's temple and the discoloration around it, I realized what made it so unsettling. It wasn't the wound as much as it was that there was extra makeup on it to hide it.

I addressed the attendant, "Sir, I know you must use make up, but children don't wear makeup. Do you think you might have a band-aid?" I explained that Will would have proudly shown off his *boo-boo* to anyone, just like a soldier wears his badges and medals.

He immediately smiled, nodded in agreement, and replied, "We will get him one."

I was later told that one of the workers from the funeral home ran down the street to a doctor's office and quickly brought back snoopy band-aids. There! Will's snoopy boo-boo strip was in place on his temple. It was just the right thing to do.

My dear family and close friends said their goodbyes. It was the last time I would get to care for the gift from God that HE had knit together under my heart, in my secret place (Psalm 139), but I was still not ready to say good-bye. I have never said it to this day not even in my heart. You see, I know what I saw, felt, and heard and experienced in Heaven. When I see Will again, I will look into those dancing brown eyes, and it will be as though no time has passed. I simply believe it with all my heart -- because I have been there, too. Will is now on his own spiritual adventure.

VII

God's People

"A new commandment I give to you, that you love one another: just as I have loved you, you also are to love one another."

John 13: 34 (ESV)

I realize that to know what to say during a tragedy can be difficult, as well. It still amazes me that we do not weigh our words more when people are grieving. The people who said variations of "You're young; you will have other children" need to know that there is no comfort in that thought. One may be thinking that, but by not addressing the actual loss and value of the person, one diminishes the significance of the relationship, as though children are plentiful and easily replaced as though they are merely puppies. It was very hurtful to hear that from so many people. I struggled not only with my heartache but with the insensitivity of others. I was just beginning the arduous task of life without my child.

As well-meaning Christians, we sometimes use scriptures that are better prayed than spoken because they wound instead of comfort. I will even go so far as to say, DON'T speak scripture unless you have experienced a similar trial and HE imparts it. A gentleman I greatly respected came up to me on that funeral day. In his sincere attempt to comfort me, he used a verse that wounded me deeply. It wasn't so much the quoted verse; it was more the fact it was hurtful because he had never buried a child. He got to see all his children grow up, finish school, marry, and have families of their own, as well as serve our Lord. He was living what I had hoped Will's future would be, so even in my pain, I felt such anger come over me at his lack of compassion and understanding, I lost any respect I'd had for him that day, feeling kicked while I was already down.

The body of Christ needs to learn from our mistakes. We need to encourage each other and not shoot the wounded with hard-hitting scripture bullets fired into open wounds. The scripture that is giving one person comfort may not comfort the person who is fractured by grief, especially if the loss is one that has not been personally experienced. The journey of grief is incredibly individual and unique for each person. Grief can even be irrational at times, but because of that thoughtless comment, I would vehemently want to take an Exacto knife and cut Romans 8:28 out of my Bible! *"All things work together for good for those who love God and are called for His purpose"* (NIV).

In God's time, I eventually would come to love and treasure that verse because of the deep and profound truth it holds, but I implore the reader of this book not to use God's Word carelessly. It took years of healing for me to begin to understand God and Who HE really is and to grasp the fullness and depth of meaning in that verse. It is very difficult in the death of a child to see any *good* coming from such a loss. It is the very meaning of loss in this world that will continually remind a person he/she is left with a gaping hole. It is a distinct void that is reopened with every significant milestone that will never be celebrated – not to mention every form that asks you to list your children and ages. We live to grow old and bury our parents, not our children. It is against our very sensibilities.

Over these years, I have found that it is far better to do as Jesus preached at the Sermon on the Mount, "To weep with those who weep" and to "think on things that are good and true." Treasure the memories of a precious life. I do treasure a heartfelt observation by Will's sweet young Sunday school teacher. As she struggled in her own grief for Will, she said to me, "Every week I noticed that you always made sure his socks matched his shirts." It may seem like such an insignificant comment, yet I was comforted that my love and care for Will was consistent and seen by others in the small details. She had noticed me loving and caring for my child. I just needed to hear that I was a good Mom, especially because Will was killed on *my watch*.

After the funeral, we would immediately leave to travel back to the beautiful mountain where we had walked, played, and prayed just a scant week ago. Our family and friends accompanied us to our property up in the mountains to place Will's body into the ground. This time though we would be returning to our land without our lively little boy. Bill and I knew that we wanted him to be buried up in the Blue Ridge Mountains in North Cove, North Carolina. We could only picture him buried up on the hill, just above the railroad crossing, at the entrance to our land. This was the same knoll where he sat with his daddy, looking at stars in the dark of night. This was the sacred spot where they would listen and watch for the whistle to sound and the big light from the train engine to come around the bend and thunder through the crossing as they would count the cars "1 – 2 – 3." Some trains had as many as ninety or more cars! Will was so proud of being able to count to one hundred.

We now stood around an open grave to bury a child. It was

something that had never occupied my imagination, and now it would be forever engraved into my mind's eye and in my soul. I would give final kisses to Will. Yes, we opened the casket on that beautiful hill one more time. I could hardly bear the thought of separation, not having him with me every day. Amazingly though, as I kissed him goodbye, I experienced a sense of calm and a strange glimmer of joy that was rooted deep within my soul as I remembered one day, I would see him again. Somehow, I knew what I was feeling was "the peace that passes all understanding." I knew that there was a glimmer of joy flickering weakly but bravely, and I marveled. I did think I would have to die though to ever experience joy again or, even more impossible, to have joy restored. At least I knew where Will was playing now. After all, I had experienced that brilliant destination, even if the visit was very brief.

It was final. We would have to leave our precious son's lifeless little *earth suit* behind, six feet deep in a cushioned metal box, surrounded by dirt. Standing on that beautiful mountain knoll, I couldn't put it off any longer. In my desperate smallness, I begged, *Oh Lord, I know that You can do anything! I know You can give him back! I know You are BIGGER! You can show it with a resurrection! Pleeeease! Give him back!*

The casket lid closed. Then, as if on cue, in one extraordinary moment, the roar and rumble of a train's wheels were heard on the railroad tracks, and the loud, resounding whistle blew as if in tribute to Will's young life. The long train of box and coal cars passed through the railroad crossing directly below at the base of the hill as Will's body was lowered into the ground. In that moment, God was still with us and so much BIGGER than all our grief. We had so much to learn. He had so much more to reveal.

I just wanted to go home now, but home was seven hours away. Exhaustion was setting in again. I had barely eaten all week even though I had kept my fluid intake up for the baby. After leaving the grave, we all headed just a half mile down Route 221 to a little country restaurant. I was amazed to see a huge, covered dish dinner waiting for us -- spread out and prepared by the whole community. More than seven churches had partnered together in demonstrating God's unity in love for one another as they ministered to us with meals and hospitality. The love and compassion they poured out on us was simple and genuine as they welcomed and served us along with all our family and friends that had accompanied us on the trip to the mountains. The care and great compassion of that day was like a healing salve on an open wound. Maybe we would really heal from this . . . . I could hear Will's *little boy voice* distinctly in my mind, "Be kind to one another, tenderhearted . . . ." I began to hope.

A whole community had gathered to extend sympathy and open their hearts to us. New friends would quickly become dear friends. Good and generous people who barely knew us opened their homes and let us stay overnight as their guests. How can you ever repay human kindnesses like this? A long gratitude list was growing in my heart with every kind deed, sympathetic word, and thoughtfully written card or letter. How do you ever repay such selfless giving? I will forever be in debt to the beautiful, warmhearted people of Marion and North Cove.

"We always had a song to sing." This is Linda and Bill Stapleton performing as part of their evangilistic music ministry.

VIII

God's Promise

"What a God we have! And how fortunate we are to have him, this Father of our Master Jesus! Because Jesus was raised from the dead, we've been given a brand-new life and have everything to live for, including a future in heaven -- and the future starts now! God is keeping careful watch over us and the future. The Day is coming when you'll have it all -- life healed and whole. I know how great this makes you feel, even though you have to put up with every kind of aggravation in the meantime. Pure gold put in the fire comes out of it proved pure; genuine faith put through this suffering comes out proved genuine. When Jesus wraps this all up, it's your faith, not your gold that God will have on display as evidence of his victory."

1 Peter 1: 3-7 (NIV)

Letters and notes poured in. Somehow, they kept me connected to reality, but as time moved forward, my guilt coupled with an overwhelming sense of obligation weighed heavily on me. I felt dead inside, and I still blamed myself. My emotions were raw and my tears always seemed ready to spill. It was as though I had only enough love and energy for the baby, and I continued to hold on to my dolly to feel comfort. I was overwhelmed and crippled by just the thought of writing thank you notes. I still had not written thank you cards for baby gifts. Now, I had so many to write for all the kindnesses shown to our family through the tragedy. I wanted to feel joyful and grateful, but instead I felt paralyzed; I couldn't move past the pain. I couldn't find stability. I felt like my heart had been placed in the casket with Will, and I knew I would never be the same. It felt like a vital part of me was gone. I wondered if this was what being an amputee felt like. I wanted to move forward, but I was missing a leg and couldn't stand up.

For the past four years Will had been my focus. All my life I had wanted to be a mother, and every day had been structured around his schedule and activities. He had just learned to zip his jacket on his own, and he was so proud of himself. He had just learned to whistle. He was fascinated in a store one day by another little boy who had mastered the art of whistling. He practiced and practiced from that day on. He was very determined, and he had gotten better and better as we walked in the woods that last weekend together. We were setting goals for learning to tie his shoes, even though I was stalling him because I was very happy with the Velcro tabs. It was getting increasingly difficult to be around our friends, all of whom had children. They still had their children! I was so angry that my child was the one whose life had been taken. I couldn't even walk through a boy's clothing department without dissolving into tears and being overwhelmed by emotions I was unable to control.

Nothing was the same in our home back in Charleston. Everything was different except for Will's room. I wouldn't let anyone touch it. Sometimes, I would go into his sunny yellow bedroom and lie on his race car bed, trying to feel or catch a sense of his presence, begging God for another visit, hoping He would let me look in on Will in that glorious place. It was easy to isolate because I felt so alone. Bill and I were trying to be so careful to not trigger the sadness in each other, that it was easier to be apart than with each other.

What kind of God are you? Who are you? How could you give so wonderfully and then take away so cruelly? I thought you were a God who loved all the children in the world. Did I really deserve this? Is this my punishment? Where was Will's guardian angel? An angel could have held back that boulder. How can this be love? I know I am to blame. I was so selfish. How could I be so selfish and stupid? Why wasn't I the one who died? I should have been in the front seat. Death would be so much better than living like this. I guess I'm not supposed to be happy in this world. I'll only be happy when I die

I could feel myself spiraling downward. My mind was in continual turmoil. The only rest stops along the way were moments with Julie, my precious little baby girl. Even with her, I doubted myself. Would I ever be able to love her as much as I loved Will? Each day caring for her needs brought a new normal. She was a helpless infant. I had to wake up, get out of bed, nurse her, change her, and so on. Going through the motions of *life*, I was coping, but the emotional energy it took drained me. The pain of the hell I was living in felt as though I was carrying the weight of the world, and I wondered if I would ever be healed.

With the holidays fast approaching, my parents decided that Bill and I needed to come *home*. I knew they were concerned and felt helpless when they saw the fragility of our emotional state. Bill was coping by staying busy, but his breakdowns were dramatic and frequent. He was in contact with the police a lot and dealing with the car. I was so sad and withdrawn. I could feel everyone tiptoeing around me. We were both so broken that we couldn't help each other.

Going home meant traveling back to Ocean City, New Jersey. Bill and I had grown up and met there, but we loved living in the South. New Jersey didn't feel like home anymore. We felt displaced and disoriented. Nothing felt normal. Life did not feel like it fit us anymore. But with Mom and Dad's persuasion, we packed up the rental car and went *home for the holidays.*

Thanksgiving arrived. I did not feel very thankful. I felt broken and empty. This was the time of the year when my family all sat around a huge, abundantly set table to thank our God for His bountiful blessings. But this year -- one was missing -- and so missed. I made myself concentrate on the things I could be truly thankful for: both our children were not dead, and that I would see Will again. The horror of the explosion and the noises of the incident randomly flashed back often in my mind, and I would run into my safe dark room where I would calm myself and stand in the little beam of light, looking up and remembering that Will was in Heaven and that Julie had been spared by God with the handle on that infant carrier. Julie needed me the most now. Will was living with Jesus and having the time of his life.

Even amid a loving family, I felt so alone in the depth of my loss. Intellectually, I knew they were hurting too, but if I couldn't even help myself, how could I help them? The hole in my life changed everything. I could not reconcile the emotion of my pain with the contrast of the expectations of upcoming joy in the holiday season either. This was Will's favorite time of year – his fourth birthday on December 5th, and then right around the corner was Christmas!

To ignore the pain or pretend it wasn't there was more exhausting than to pretend joy or happiness. I had no emotional energy to pretend or wear a mask. To live true to myself I had to live in the reality of the truth. The truth being that my heart was hemorrhaging every day. My spirit was broken; I was broken. The days were filled with the routine. My life revolved around meeting the needs of the baby.

On the heels of Thanksgiving, the Christmas season soon arrived. I didn't want to shop or bake or go to Christmas gatherings and celebrations. It's the children that make Christmas so special. Everyone around me had their children to tuck in their beds. It took too much energy to fight the downward pull of sadness, and I would find myself curled up in my bed, a ball of self-pity before I knew what was happening.

My family tried to go through the motions and do all the traditional festivities to lighten the somber mood. But truthfully, it is just easier to isolate. It was so hard for everyone, even though pouring our love and attention on the precious *remaining* child did bring a measure of comfort. I would watch as Julie was passed around like some live, little love machine, seemingly unaffected by the tragic event. Almost five months-old now, she was delightful! She was everyone's little love bucket to pour their pain into. She loved to cuddle and snuggle, and she simply spilled out love and laughter. Her little life comforted us as we all tried to reconcile the pain of the gaping hole within our hearts.

Bill stayed busy with the details of our everyday life. He was a small business owner, his piano teaching and tuning business was in South Carolina, so there was no income while we stayed in New Jersey. Because Will was wearing a seat belt when he died, some money was given to us through our insurance company, which helped Bill's anxiety level. He was in continual contact with the attorney, the police, friends, students, and customers. It brought comfort to him but seemed to further the distance between us. He was caught up in the busyness of life. I, on the other hand, didn't want to talk to anyone. I was content to let the world go by. I was frustrated and annoyed with the press. I didn't want to ride the *merry-go-round* of the murder anymore. Ordinary, day-to-day living was hard enough for me. My deep sadness and grief were moving me toward depression, but at the time, no one ever really mentioned that word. Grief would be the dark abyss for me. The pain! I wasn't sure I even wanted to live! Living was too hard! I would fantasize about playing hide and seek with Will in Heaven. I doubted my sanity. I am so glad I wrote down that trip to Heaven, but in my state of mind, I began to frequently entertain the thoughts of leaving this life and going back there.

It would be nearly Christmas before we were intimate again. "I need you honey," Bill pleaded. "Even when we are alone, you are somewhere else. I miss Will too, but we need to move forward."

Bill went on to question my *lack of interest* and *my lack of needing to feel comfort from him.* I couldn't pretend anything anymore! Experiencing the reality of the harshness of life changed me in a way I could not have foreseen. Tragedy doesn't make one different; tragedy reveals who one really is. Bill and I already had problems in our relationship. I already felt alone in my marriage. I didn't have any strength to expend energy to pretend something I didn't feel. Before Will's death, the *people pleaser* inside of me went to great lengths to keep him happy. But now, I was done. I was doing all I could do to hold myself together. I didn't want him to need me. It felt like more pressure than I could carry.

I was already carrying the heaviest burdens a person could carry -- guilt and shame. Bill couldn't comfort me. From the night that he had blamed me to the present, he had not repeated it; he didn't need to because I blamed myself even more. The weight of the guilt and shame drained me of any value I had for myself. I was guilty! I was to blame! I didn't deserve to feel good! I was worthless as a human being! I believed that my selfish decision those fifteen years earlier had brought this on us. Yes, I should have died! I should have been in the front passenger seat, not Will. *God, you are so cruel!* I did believe that I would have to die, too if I were ever to be happy again. I was done faking anything. I could never be good enough. I vowed I would never, ever pretend anymore. I knew the religious people around me would judge me, but I didn't care anymore. It just took too much energy.

Carried by God's grace we made it through Christmas. As I look back over those photos taken for Julie's first Christmas, I see my forced smile on the face of a shell of a person. No real-time memories of anything but a cuddly sweet baby over-shadowed by numbness and unspeakable pain.

Shortly after Christmas, Bill headed back to South Carolina without me. He had to return the rental car, buy a car, and get back to his students. He needed to get back into the routine of work. He wanted me to come with him, but I refused -- and I didn't care. I felt like a deflated balloon. He wanted more of me than I could give. I was not a good person. I would never measure up. I just wanted to be cared for, surrounded by my loving family. Mom and Dad provided unspoken security and unconditional love. I couldn't even imagine being away from them at this point. I had been married fourteen years and out of the family home all these years, yet in my heartache, I became their child again.

It was two weeks into January when Bill called, "You need to come home, Lin. The case is going to trial next week."

I was shocked, numb, and still raw with grief. I didn't want to go back to South Carolina. I didn't want to leave New Jersey. I needed my family. It had only been two and a half months since Will's death! I didn't want to make sure justice was done! I didn't care if two teenagers got tried as adults or not! I didn't care! I only wanted Will back. I wanted a *do-over.* I didn't want to move forward. I wanted to curl up in the bed, pull the covers up over my head, and stay there until the pain, heaviness, and sickness went away. It took all the energy I had to take care of the baby! Going back to where I would have to care for us all by myself terrified me! I did not want to try to rebuild our lives without the support of my family. I did not want to face the emptiness and loneliness I felt inside. I would have to go back to our home, a home where there would be no more little boy noises or adventure filled messes -- no more little Will.

Even though I was screaming and kicking inside my soul, I would do the right thing and be the obedient, responsible, compliant, first-born child and go back to my marriage and life in South Carolina. Within a few days, my mother and I packed our suitcases and flew back to South Carolina. It was Julie's first plane ride. I had carefully marked it in her baby book. *Hmmmm,* I darkly mused, as *I facetiously wondered where they put the "baby's first murder trial" sticker?*

Bill met us at the then, tiny Charleston airport. I felt emotionless when I saw him. I hadn't even missed him. It was easier to stay detached than to allow the pain of the ever-present guilt and shame to surface and cloud my thoughts. Now, I felt even guiltier. I was a cruel, bad person. I was the stranger. A big part of me was gone. I continued to go through the motions. Bill kissed me and held me tight. I knew he needed me, but I was missing in action, post-partum depression, grief, and post-homicide stress. All I knew was that I didn't know how to get back to him or to myself.

It was easier at the present to abdicate responsibility for my life to Bill and my mother. Bill was manic and persistent. He seemed to be on automatic pilot. He seemed to always be doing something. He would do whatever he needed to do. He just needed to keep himself busy. In contrast, I had only enough energy and focus to care for the baby as my mother cared for us all.

I had no expectations for the trial. I had already surrendered that to God and the authorities. It seemed easy to trust God. After all, HE had already said, "I am BIGGER." I held onto HIS voice in my head a lot. It helped calm my soul as each day melted into another, and I went through the motions of daily life.

There had been quite a public outcry in the newspapers in South Carolina, cries for justice! The public was outraged. The people identified with us because it could have been any one of them on that road with their families. As I think back to that time of 1986 going into 1987, there were just glimpses of cell phones and Internet. If this incident had happened today, it would have likely gone viral. Bill and I knew, though, that with God's perspective, it wasn't as random as it appeared. We knew that there is always a God-view. We were being held in HIS hands and that God had the BIGGER plan. We did not believe in coincidences. We believed in God-incidences.

Just like the story of Job in the Bible, we were in the spiritual battle of our faith. As it was, there were many news articles giving voice for the boys and for the state's responsibility. Under South Carolina law, a person is deemed an adult at the age of seventeen. If a person younger than seventeen is charged with a crime, the case is tried in the family courts, which generally are not opened to the public. Meanwhile, during our stay in New Jersey through the holidays, the state had been working hard to determine justice in our son's murder. There had already been a hearing for the boys to be tried as adults.

According to an article published in *The State* newspaper, the state solicitor had scheduled a hearing for the boys right before Christmas on December 17, 1986. Family Court J Judge Jeff D. Griffin listened to the Eleventh Court Solicitor Donald V. Myers petition the court for both boys to be tried as adults in the general circuit court because the crime was committed in "an extremely violent manner," and they noted that Robert McIlvain had been previously treated as an adult by both the courts and the school system. The judge pointed out that McIlvain had been allowed to drop out of school with the blessing of family courts, hold down a job as a sheetrock worker, and generally associate with older people. The Department of Youth Services considered McIlvain a youth who could not be rehabilitated in the *juvenile justice system.*

Curtis Iriel, seventeen, was already charged with murder and assault, but Robert McIlvain, sixteen, was in custody of family court. Myers wanted them both tried as adults because of the seriousness of the crime and because a single trial would be easier on the court system. At the two-hour waiver hearing, Judge Griffith heard statements by both suspects in which each blamed the other for the incident. McIlvain's statement said that he and Iriel were walking on the Leaphart Road overpass on I-26 when Iriel spotted a large rock and said, "I'm going to throw this off the bridge on the highway."

McIlvain said, "I said, 'man, you're crazy.'" He also continued stating that he heard Iriel say, "Man, let's have some

Pretrial headlines in various
newspapers.

fun by throwing rocks off the bridge."

In the first two statements Iriel made to detectives, both of which were read in court, Iriel blamed the deed on McIlvain. "Bobby McIlvain saw a big rock and said, 'Let's throw that big rock off the bridge.' He picked up the rock and pushed it off the bridge. I did not help him."

This was the first statement and made about an hour after the incident. But Iriel gave a different account to detectives a few minutes later. In the later statement, he said, "We picked up a large rock. I was going to throw the rock on an eighteen-wheeler (truck). I slid the rock over the rail. I saw a car coming, and I tried to catch the rock, but it was too late."

Iriel's second statement indicated that the incident "started as a joke but turned into an accident, killing someone." During the hearing, Scarborough, the attorney for the prosecution, asked Detective P.C. Faglie whether he had any way of knowing which statement was true? Faglie replied that he didn't.

Scarborough also asked Faglie whether he thought Iriel could have lifted the boulder himself. "Is it your opinion that it would probably take two people to carry that rock that far?"

"Yes sir. We do not believe that Curtis Iriel toted that rock and threw it off the bridge by himself," said Faglie.

McIlvain did not testify at the hearing but sat at a small table, fidgeting and tugging at the sleeves of his plaid work shirt. During the hearing, Hubert Eaker, a psychologist for the State Department of Youth Services (DYS), took the stand. He said McIlvain had an IQ of 72, a little above the mentally retarded level. He also said McIlvain could not read or write and suffered from an inferiority complex.

In Scarborough's closing argument to the judge, he said,

"The public is crying out for some sort of redress of the wrongs done to the Stapleton family. They were just driving down the highway. This could have happened to anyone -- to you or to me."

Scarborough said the DYS report on McIlvain found little chance of his being rehabilitated, and that "the public interest would best be served by keeping Bobby McIlvain off the streets for as long as possible." The family court judge ruled that sixteen-year-old Robert McIlvain should be tried as an adult.

Donald Myers said he was pleased Judge Griffin had transferred the case and that "This was the first hurdle to overcome; the next thing is for us to get in and start evaluating the case."

Myers also stated that the Lexington County Grand Jury will have to determine whether prosecutors have enough evidence to warrant the time and expense of a trial. Both boys had been charged with murder, but other charges, including three counts of assault and battery with intent to kill and one count of malicious damage to property were likely to be brought for the Grand Jury 's consideration.

With all the legalities out of the way, the State of South Carolina moved forward to prosecute two teenagers in the malicious murder of our son. Because we had been out of the state, everything seemed to be moving with uncharacteristic speed in the judicial process. Bill, my mother, the baby, and I, along with our close friend, Lee, headed to Columbia. The murder trial was about to begin.

IX

God's Power

God had gone before us. In only fifty workdays, over three major holidays --Thanksgiving, Christmas, and New Year -- a full murder trial had been assembled. The public's outcry for justice brought the spotlight to Lexington County Courthouse in West Columbia, South Carolina. On January 19, 1987, the headline in the newspaper read "Teen Will Testify for Prosecution." Sixteen-year-old Robert McIlvain would testify for the State in the trial of Curtis Iriel, who had been charged with murder and assault and battery with intent to kill.

Eleventh Circuit Solicitor Donald V. Myers said he agreed to allow McIlvain to plead guilty to one count of accessory after the fact of murder in exchange for his testimony. McIlvain had not been charged in connection with the death because he was a juvenile. Also, because he was a juvenile, he was originally charged with murder in family court, but a recent ruling said he would be tried as an adult; however, those charges were put on hold to allow him the opportunity to testify for the State (Feeley).

As witnesses for the prosecution, we would get front row seats, while we experienced how our justice system worked. As we sat through the jury selection, I found myself both detached and ambivalent. I couldn't imagine feeling any better no matter what the jury decided. Nothing was going to bring Will back. I was particularly touched by the thoughtfulness of the courthouse personnel throughout the courthouse. They were so helpful, even setting aside a room near the courtroom so that our family could have some privacy when the court was not in session. Several office personnel even watched Julie while court was in session so that my mother could experience some of the trial. We could not keep Julie in the courtroom once the trial began. Baby noises interfere with the court's recording of a case. I was glad to be able to have Julie nearby, but she was more fussy than usual; emotions in general were running high, and she seemed to sense it. Having my mother close by and a rocking chair for the baby and me helped us all calm down. Thoughtful kindnesses demonstrated amid the stress have never been forgotten. The respect and compassion extended to our whole family over those days in the courthouse honored us deeply. We were truly grateful.

Up to this point, we had not seen the two boys. Because we had left South Carolina and were in New Jersey, I did not even look at a newspaper or the news on TV. Of course, we knew it had been picked up by the Associated Press when it happened and had been on the television news, but it was not until my return and present at the trial that I began to realize the impact of our family's tragedy and how extensive the coverage had been in

South Carolina. Not only because it was so senseless and random, but also because of the previous court ruling to try both boys together as adults. Prior to the trial, Circuit Judge Hubert Long was asked by the defense to move Iriel's case out of Lexington County because of the wide-spread publicity the incident received in the Midlands. Pat McWhirter, public defender, was quoted as saying, "I'm going to ask him (the judge) to move it to Timbuktu because that's just about the only place where no one has heard about this case" (Hook)!

The jury selection was fascinating. The actual process was done methodically and carefully. There were so many quality people, and their differences and the questions that were asked brought me to a new level of appreciation for our justice system. Both Bill and I were satisfied with the final selection of jurors and prayed for each of them. After a full morning of jury selection and a break for lunch, we then came back into the courtroom and waited for the trial to begin.

It was not until we sat waiting for the prosecutor and defense attorney to make their opening remarks that it dawned on me, *I would be in the same room with the boys*. I did not feel prepared, and I could feel a wave of anxiety swelling up in me. I had not anticipated this moment at all, and, quite honestly, I did not know how I would react when faced with the boys who killed Will. Up to this point, they were only names to me.

It came time for the police officers to escort the defendant, Jimmy Curtis Iriel, into the courtroom and seat him at the table for the defense. I stared directly at Jimmy Curtis Iriel across the room. He boldly returned my stare, but through me at the same time. Dark and stony, emotionless and cold, we made no connection, except the fact that I recognized the face immediately.

I was stunned! It was the face of Satan from the vision I had in the emergency room! The same face on the figure of Satan wearing the black robe, as he was cradling the rock like a baby. The very same face the night Will died! I sat back stunned!

Considering what I had been reading and studying about Job in the Bible, it made sense. The evil one, Satan, was the *real* enemy. God had used this young man's face to put a face to the sinister act of violence in the *BIGGER* picture of the spiritual realm. I was trying in my mind to make sense of all this. On one hand, God was clearly identifying Satan as the true enemy. From the beginning of time, Satan has been on his own mission to steal, kill, and destroy (John 10:10, NLT)! But God was also reminding me of the other half of the verse: *"I have come that you may have life and have it to the full."*

All evil done in this world is instigated by the "Prince of the air." I remembered that verse again from that fateful night on the interstate. *"He roams around like a roaring lion seeking those he can devour."* Satan is allowed, yet always limited, by Almighty God, who is also his Creator (Isaiah 54, KJV). Only HE knows all those involved in every situation. Only HE knows the outcome and purpose within one's journey. Only HE knows how to turn our tragedy into victory. I believe God uses every circumstance to teach us and move us toward a greater purpose. It would only be through our faith in Him that we could overcome this heartache.

I tapped Bill's arm beside me and whispered to him that Curtis Iriel was the face of Satan. I felt like I was passing on a revelation, but Bill didn't seem surprised at all. He whispered back, "Makes sense. This is God's battle, not ours. God is BIGGER."

Even as I write this, I marvel again, that even though Bill and I were two distinct people, grieving differently in our individual pain, we were joined by God through our spirits. He never doubted me, not even once, when it came to spiritual things. God was carrying us both and empowering us together with His supernatural strength. Donald Myers, the solicitor and prosecuting attorney for the State of South Carolina, said in his opening remarks to the jury, "This trial is going to come down to one thing: malice -- wickedness and whether someone is devoid of any social feeling for a fellow human being" (O'Boyle).

That set the tone for the trial. Exhibit A entered the full courtroom on a truck dolly. The massive 189-pound slab of granite was dramatically rolled in and placed in front of the jury box and judge for all to see. The slab was eighteen inches wide, twenty-eight inches long, and five inches thick.

Public Defender Mike Kolb said in his opening argument that the prosecution would be unable to prove Iriel was on the overpass when the boulder was pushed from the guardrail. "We have evidence that he might not have done this," he stated (Feeley).

The crime was then reconstructed through diagrams of the overpass and road and photos of the mangled car seat into which Will had been strapped. We were thankful that photos of Will's lifeless body had been ruled inadmissible by Judge Hubert Long. One of the videos shown revealed the difficult struggle that two husky State Law Enforcement Division agents had as they tried to remove the boulder from the rear seat of the car.

The condition of the car was best described by reporter Sally McInerney in her column, "Cola Town" dated November 13, 1986:

> The garage door is open revealing a light
> beige Chrysler It is a knee-weakening

sight. The front windshield has a gaping hole in it. Square bits of shatter-proof glass barely hang on to what little is left of the windshield. Inside, the rearview mirror hangs like a small, sad chandelier. The little boy's car seat has been jerked hard to the left, and circles of deep red blood splotch the arm rest, an [*American Greetings*] anniversary card and a roadmap. The car floor is littered with glass. The green-cloth ceiling is ripped from front to back by one long tear. The back glass is broken out. William Richard Stapleton Jr. died in this mess.… (*The Columbia Record*)

P.C. Faglie testified. He was the Lexington investigator for the case who arrived on the scene within minutes.

It was not a good feeling. I have seen a lot of things in law enforcement. I've seen homicides. I've seen car wrecks. But when you see something like that …. It's something very, very . . . well the little boy was still in the car. His father was on the side of the road praying. The mother, she was just getting out of the car from the back seat. She was holding the little girl. (Feeley)

Sheriff Metts took the witness stand:

It's a miracle that the mother, father,

and infant daughter, Julie, survived. The granite boulder, shaped somewhat like a suitcase, slashed through the car upright rather than on one of its flat sides. It is now lying on a concrete floor in the garage next to the car. You cannot budge it, and so, officers also say, it was a miracle that the mother was able to move this massive hunk of rock off her baby girl, which is where it finally landed. But it is hard to think of anything like this as a miracle. Initially there was hope that it was an accident. Maybe the report on the radio was wrong? Maybe it was something that somehow fell and was not pushed? Devastation was the mood in the emergency room where the little boy's body was taken, according to a pediatrician, and perplexity remains the feeling at the sheriff's department (Feeley).

Other officers said the teens were taken into custody within an hour of the incident. The boys reacted to the news that a child had died, as if it were no big deal. They treated the whole thing like a joke. Iriel was without conscience, as though he had no soul. He told officers his home address was the bathroom of a grocery store.

"When they say something like that," Faglie said, "you know something went wrong way, way, down the line" (Feeley).

The diagrams revealed the boulder *traveled* about sixty feet to the point where it was dropped. About halfway across the Leaphart Bridge, you can easily see the deep grooves where the boulder was pushed along the railing until it got to the place where it was dropped. There was also expert testimony to the fact the weight of the boulder, the speed the car was traveling, and the *drop* from the overpass had been sent to experts to be calculated for the impact to the car, concluding that the force of the boulder's impact was the equivalent of a stick of dynamite going off!

At the time, I thought, *no wonder Bill had suffered temporary hearing loss*! (At the time of the trial, we had no idea that Julie had sustained profound total hearing loss in her right ear during the incident. We would find out a few years later through her growth development that all the little hairs in her cochlea were sheared off from the force of the explosion on that fateful night.)

Bill's testimony came before mine. Bill testified that he was driving, and the rock crashed through the windshield, tore the roof of the car, and smashed the rear window before coming to rest in the back seat.

"The first thing I thought was that I hit a wall. My glasses were knocked off, and my second thought was there had been an explosion in the car. Then I saw the hole in the windshield of the car. My wife woke up and said, 'Oh, God, oh, God, what happened?'" (Hook*)*.

He continued to describe that night and said that he realized his son was dead. "I didn't tell my wife right away. I didn't want to upset her. But his (son's) mouth was full of blood. He wasn't responding . . . he was gone." Bill's voice cracked as he fought back the tears while he described for the seven-women, five-men jury how he and I knelt beside the interstate and began praying for our son. "This was very hard" *(Hook)*.

My time on the stand was mercifully brief, and it affirmed all that Bill had stated previously.

> Mrs. Stapleton testified briefly
> Monday, prefacing her testimony
> with, 'By the grace of God, I'm here
> to talk to you.' She explained her
> and her husband's frantic efforts to
> get the boulder off their four-
> month-old daughter in the rear
> seat. 'The baby was screaming. She
> was hurt, and I couldn't get that rock
> off. I said, "Oh God, what's wrong?"'
> (O'Boyle)

After we testified, I was able to relax more. We would return the next day to hear from each of the boys. They would be called on to testify and be cross examined. We were looking forward to their testimonies because we were told that each one narrated a very different version of the story.

The younger boy, Robert (*Bobby*), had become the State's key evidence. He became an eyewitness testifying for the prosecution. McIlvain, who was never charged in the case, had agreed to plead guilty to accessory charges in exchange for prosecutors not charging him with murder. He would face a ten-year maximum sentence to just tell the truth. Since Bobby was a young man who was mentally challenged, some might say he was *slow*, he had been in special education classes until he dropped out of school in ninth grade. He became a good witness for the State because he gave a most compelling testimony. Because of his lack of mental acumen, his testimony was child-like and understandably believable.

It was especially enlightening when he said, "I knew I was acting bad with him, but I decided to help anyway." McIlvain said, "I removed my shoes and socks and put my socks on my hands. I didn't want my fingerprints on the rock" (Feeley).

"One could hear the unified gasp in the courtroom at the realization that here was a young boy without guile, only recounting the truth. He did not have the sophistication to make those details up or manipulate the facts. He would continue to vividly recount the moments leading up to Will's horrific death" (Feeley).

He continued to describe to a deathly silent courtroom how he helped Iriel roll the 189- pound boulder end-over-end to the overpass. At one point, he decided he'd had enough. He testified, "I hollered at him to get the rock out of the road. I knew he was going to do something with it. I told him, 'Man, you're crazy if you do it!' Iriel replied, 'Ah, you just don't want to have fun.'" McIlvain watched as Iriel put a *bear hug* on the slab of granite and flipped it up to the guardrail of Leaphart Road overpass on I-26. "It's your blood, not mine," McIlvain said as he started to walk away. "Then I heard a sound like a loud crash, like glass breaking. I looked back, and I didn't see the rock," McIlvain recalled and then added, "I heard him shout 'good shot' when he dropped the boulder." As they ran away, McIlvain asked Iriel why he did it. "He said, 'Let's get the hell out of here. Don't worry about it'" (O'Boyle).

Jimmy Curtis Iriel confidently took the stand after

McIlvain. He acted as if we were the ones who were making a big thing out of nothing. His testimony could be characterized as ridiculous if the situation had not been so tragic. He started off by saying that neither he nor McIlvain were on the overpass when the boulder hit the car. He spoke one lie after another. He pointed at the 189-pound boulder in front of the jury box and stated, "This is the first time I've ever seen that rock, the first time in my life" (Hook).

Myers's voice, laced with incredulity, shouted at Iriel during cross-examination and called him a liar several times. Myers read testimony that Iriel had given previously to investigators where he said that he had "dragged the boulder along the overpass guard rail" to position it better over passing traffic. Then, when investigators took Iriel to the overpass, the scratch marks were confirmed and visible on the guardrail. Myers shouted at Iriel, "You made up something that was a lie? But it actually happened" (Hook).

Iriel admitted he gave statements to Detective Yarborough and Deputy Grice, saying that he pushed the boulder onto the car but said the confessions were coerced out of him. "I was scared and in shock, but they just kept bothering me with questions. It was about 3 a.m. when they questioned me, and I was tired and sleepy. I just signed them to get them off my back," he said (O'Boyle).

But on cross-examination, a visibly angered Myers screamed at Iriel and called him a liar several times. "The detectives read you your rights, didn't they? If you say they didn't, it's a lie" (O'Boyle).

"That confession was a lie. I made it all up because I was shocked and scared," Iriel cockily retorted" (O'Boyle).

A police officer measures and examines the actual
189-pound boulder that was thrown off the bridge
and hit the Stapleton car.

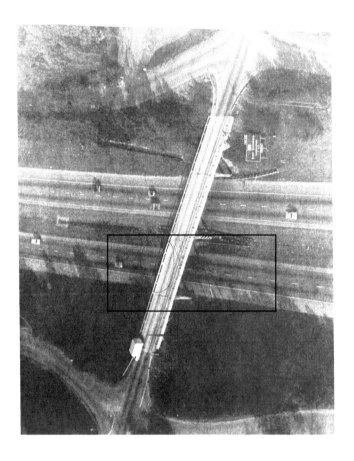

This aerial shot taken by the police shows the overpass and the highway below -- the actual crime scene. There is a faint circle on the bridge indicating from where the boulder was thrown.

Myers yelled, "Are you telling this jury that you made up a story that turned out to be true? Are those marks on the railing imaginary? Is what's left of that car imaginary? I don't have any more questions for you!" Myers sat down in frustration with a red face and the veins on his neck visible (O'Boyle).

Iriel's court-appointed attorney, Mike Kolb, asked Judge Long to dismiss murder charges against Iriel because the prosecution hadn't proved that he had intended to kill someone. One statement Iriel made to investigators but later denied was that he had intended to drop the boulder on a tractor trailer.

"I think at best they have a case of involuntary manslaughter," Kolb said.

Involuntary manslaughter is the legal term for killing someone accidently. Negligence and disregard for others are elements of the crime. Judge Long said there was more than enough evidence for the jury to rule that Iriel intended to hurt someone with the huge boulder. "This is no different from putting poison in a can of Carnation milk, having it bought and fed to a baby and then saying you didn't mean to kill that particular child," the judge said. "That rock was calculated to kill. It was just as dangerous as a gun. Whether it was meant for an eighteen-wheeler or not makes no difference. Truck drivers value their lives, too," Long said. Pointing toward Bill and me, he continued. "This fine couple lost their child. His skull was crushed to pieces!" Judge Long denied the request to drop murder charges and left the question for the jury to decide (O'Boyle).

During the second day of the trial, the Lexington County jurors said they wanted to see the scene of the crime, the I-26 overpass for themselves. The fourteen jurors were taken by van to the Leaphart Road overpass in West Columbia. Bill joined the prosecution team and the jurors as they went there. I chose to stay behind at the courthouse with the baby and my mother. I was emotionally exhausted, and I so wanted this all to be over. I knew it was going to turn out the way that God decreed.

The Sheriff's deputies and the red-coated court bailiffs blocked traffic so that the twelve jurors and two alternate jurors could examine the guardrails on the Leaphart Road I-26 Overpass. Several eighteen-wheeler trucks blew their horns at those looking down. As the jurors looked down at the cars and trucks passing underneath, they were aware of how close they were to the traffic. They could see items sitting on people's front seats. As the wind whipped through their hair, they knew those boys must have realized the potential for tragedy. It was not a rock or a pebble; it was a 189-pound granite boulder! It was a bone-chilling site as they looked at the three-foot-long scratch marks made by the boulder at the base of a concrete guardrail, still clearly visible after these seventy-five days since the crime. Evil stood there on that night of November 5, 1986.

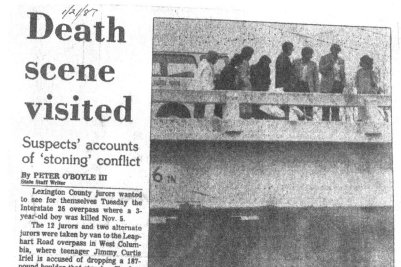

Death scene visited

Suspects' accounts of 'stoning' conflict

By PETER O'BOYLE III
State Staff Writer

Lexington County jurors wanted to see for themselves Tuesday the Interstate 26 overpass where a 3-year-old boy was killed Nov. 5.

The 12 jurors and two alternate jurors were taken by van to the Leaphart Road overpass in West Columbia, where teenager Jimmy Curtis Iriel is accused of dropping a 187-pound boulder that struck a Charleston family's car and killed William Stapleton Jr.

I detached from the trial by tending to Julie's simple needs, insulating emotionally from the drama of the murder trial; again, I was just moving through the motions. I was being held tightly; I could feel a supernatural peace. It wasn't me. I was too weak. It was something so much *BIGGER* than me. My heart ached to be holding my son again, and yet I believed and trusted that God knew my innermost pain and was holding me instead. The real enemy had already been defeated by Jesus long ago. I knew I was on the winning side; I just didn't know how I would ever be able to go on without our little boy and carry the guilt I felt.

Court reconvened. The testimony coming from a mentally challenged youth was too compelling. In a short but impassioned closing argument, Solicitor Donald Myers told the jurors they would have to decide whether Iriel showed malice when he dropped the boulder off the overpass. Malice, when it is used in court, describes a person with *an evil intent, a heart bent on evil.*

"Does this not have the stench of murder, the aroma of malice on it when it's thrown off a bridge?" Myers asked as he pointed to the boulder. "Does someone who drops something like this on the head of a three-year-old care about the consequences? Or does he just have wickedness and malicious mischief in his heart?" Myers asked. "This should never have happened. Will Stapleton should be home in Charleston rather than in a grave!" Myers said he would do everything in his power to see that Iriel never had a chance to throw anything off an overpass again (O'Boyle).

When the closing arguments came, there was a part of me that felt sad for the boys and their families. Ours were not the only lives changed forever. I was sure that their lives would never be the same either.

X

God's Punitive Sovereignty

"But I say to you, love your enemies, bless those who curse
you, do good to those who hate you, and pray for those who
spitefully use you and persecute you, that you maybe sons of
your Father in Heaven; for He makes the sun rise on the evil
and on the good, and sends rain on the just and the unjust."

Matthew 5:44-45 (NIV)

"A saint is never consciously a saint – a saint is consciously
dependent on God."

Oswald Chambers

We would recess until a verdict was reached. The Lexington County jurors deliberated only one and a half hours before ruling that Jimmy Curtis Iriel was the person who pushed the huge slab of granite off the Leaphart Road overpass onto our family's car, killing Will. He was found guilty of first-degree murder, three counts of assault and battery with intent to kill, and malicious injury to personal property in connection with death.

Circuit Judge Hubert Long ruled that to save us all from coming back to court another day for sentencing, he would save our family from more pain and anguish and also save the State some money and sentence both boys on the same day. He called for a brief recess so that McIlvain could be brought from the jail to the courthouse. Unfamiliar with court procedures, this whole ordeal had been a fast-learning experience for us. We had no idea that the judge could even do something like that! Sentencing would take place on the same day as the verdict. After a recess for lunch, the court quickly re-assembled. We took our now-familiar seats behind the prosecutor.

The proceedings started with Bobby McIlvain and his attorney approaching the bench to plead guilty to the charge of accessory to the murder. My heart was moved by the sight of Bobby's mother. She obviously was unprepared for the unexpected sentencing and had rushed to come straight from her place of work. My heart broke for this single mother of nine children dressed in her housekeeping uniform, standing near her son in a packed courtroom while his future was to be determined. I felt compassion for this worn nervous little lady standing in front of the tall judge's bench nervously twisting the edges of her apron. On this day lives would never, ever be the same, because of an evil heartless, malicious act of violence. We shared the cost of heartache.

I was very surprised when Judge Hubert Long looked up from the proceedings and addressed us directly from the bench.

"Mr. and Mrs. Stapleton, before we go any further, I want to take a few moments to hear what you have to say. I have heard many exemplary comments from the people who have gotten to know you as they worked on this case. They talk about what fine people you are. Your strength and faith have touched all of us. I am respectfully asking if you would address the court as to what you would like me to do with these boys."

Bill and I came forward to address the court. In a moving and dramatic courtroom speech with his left arm around me and his right hand holding his Bible, Bill opened his comments by thanking the Judge and acknowledging the court. His opening statement after is forever in my mind:

"We are no different than anyone else in this courtroom. We just happen to believe that God's Word is the ultimate authority, and in the Bible, it says that 'it rains on the just and on the unjust,' (Matthew 5:45 KJV). We can thank and give praise to our Lord in all of this because we had our *spiritual raincoats* on. We know that Will is with Jesus, and one day we will see him again. But for now, we want you to know that we can forgive you because God has forgiven us. He sent Jesus, His son, to pay for your sin and all the sins in this world. This is from the heart; I am praying for your soul, and my wife is praying for your soul. I love you, and I pray for you. I don't know what was in your mind that day, but if my little boy was here today, he would forgive you as I do."

Bobby McIlvain, who had been standing with his lawyer, approached us, and reached out to shake Bill's hand in gratitude. Bill, instead, put his arms around Bobby and hugged him. Bobby started to weep and say how sorry he was repeatedly. Several jurors began to cry.

Looking across the court, toward Curtis Iriel, Bill said, "I love you; I love you; do you hear me?"

I will always remember the court officer jerking the slumped Curtis Iriel up by his collar into a standing position, so he would look back at Bill as he spoke to him.

"There wasn't a dry eye in the courtroom," Solicitor Myers later said (O'Boyle).

Bill and I had no idea we would get to address the court that day. When I heard Bill say, "We forgive you" to the boys, it made me examine my own thoughts. Up to that point, I hadn't

When the verdicts were announced, the news
was everywhere.

consciously given much thought to the subject of forgiveness because my emotions were too raw. As I stood beside him, I thought to myself, *He's speaking for me; do I forgive them too? Yes!* I knew deep in my heart that I did! I really did! I am so glad that God gave us that amazing opportunity to glorify Him in a way that was beyond our understanding.

Judge Long had indicated he was leaning toward sentencing McIlvain to adult prison but said he was touched by his spontaneous repentant actions. The judge also spoke to Bill and me by saying, "You really exemplify what Christ stood for: love, love for your neighbor." To our relief, he sentenced Robert McIlvain to serve six years in the Aiken Youth Correction Center (O'Boyle).

Up until the very end, Curtis Iriel had refused to say why he had dropped the boulder off the overpass. As he stood emotionless with a slight smirk on his face, he declined to say anything about the crime before Judge Long sentenced him. Ultimately, Judge Hubert Long had the last word, and he had plenty to say when sentencing Iriel.

"Young man, the crime you committed is the most heinous thing imaginable." Judge Long was visibly angry. "There is nothing more callous, more insensitive, more lacking in regard for others than to take a rock of this size and throw it on a car. You were not drunk. You weren't on cocaine. You were just totally full of the devil. It is the most senseless thing I've ever seen. You crushed that child's brain to pieces! I'm going to make it as hard for you to get out of jail as I can. What you have done cannot be tolerated. It's absolutely essential that we be able to drive on the highways without having to look up at every overpass to see if someone is going to drop a rock." He also addressed the jury by saying, "I agree with your verdict. You could have done absolutely nothing different. The evidence was overwhelming."

Jimmy Curtis Iriel was sentenced to life plus forty years to be served consecutively in the State prison (O'Boyle).

After the sentence was handed down, Myers stated that he would work to make sure the teenager was not released from prison for the rest of his natural life. "Curtis Iriel is not fit to walk freely in society," Myers argued.

As court was finally dismissed, Judge Long said the jury would like to come down from the juror's box so they could extend their condolences to Bill and me. As the jurors surrounded us and offered hugs and handshakes, then others from the packed courtroom came forward to speak to us. I stepped back and looked up at the exquisite ceiling of the court room to acknowledge that God through the Holy Spirit was present. What I saw in the Spirit was amazingly real even to this day.

The beautiful and ornate ceiling was being rolled back like a roll of carpeting. The bluest Heavenly sky revealed a crowd of witnesses seated in a huge coliseum or type of stadium. In the center of the coliseum, standing on a Corinthian column about four feet tall, was a college age young man. I knew in my heart it was our young Will, now grown up.

He was standing on top of the column, raising both of his arms like a college cheerleader! He was grinning and motioning to the crowd of witnesses by raising his arms with every quarter, clockwise turn. North, east, south, and west, leading the cheering as the full stadium cheered! I looked around to see if anyone else had seen it but whether they did or not, there was no denying that God's glory was evident. I am still humbled by the swift justice and goodness expressed on that day. The kind, heartfelt condolences of this jury of men and women who were chosen *for such a time as this* was like a warm blanket of compassion wrapped around us.

I will always remember the brief conversation I had with Bob Rightsall, our victim's advocate, after it was all over. He had accompanied me down the hall to retrieve Julie. I had asked him why he wasn't as elated as some of the others involved in the process.

He replied soberly, "Sometimes the system works."

I looked into his eyes and saw the heaviness of his work. Realizing in that moment, the magnitude of all the people, resources, and jobs it had taken to right a wrong. Good overcame evil on this day. Bob had done his job with us and done it well. What a huge job! A job replicated, repeatedly, by thousands of civil servants in our country. God is Bigger! I was truly thankful that we had trusted God from the beginning. This was HIS story written on our lives, and it was time for us to go home.

The reporters swarmed us as we left the Lexington County Courthouse. "Were you really able to forgive the boys?" "What did you mean when you said 'I forgive you?'"

Bill was quick to reply with a clarified statement by saying, "Yes, we forgive them to free *ourselves* from bitterness, but they must still be punished by the law of the State."

The opening statement on the evening news that night was, "Father forgives boys . . . ."

Oh, Heavenly Father, thank you for using us to remind others that it is only Your love and amazing grace that is more powerful than evil.

XI

God's Portion

"For a brief moment I have forsaken you...But with everlasting
kindness I will have mercy on you."

Isaiah 54:7-8 (KJV)

*How does a person recover from the murder of a loved one? Where does
one go to find peace? How does one reconcile the past with the present? Who
are you God? What kind of God allows a child to die? Why did Will die
and not me? How does one go on living with a part of her heart gone? What
could I have done differently? Why did this happen to our family? Did we
bring this on ourselves? What do we do now? What is the next step? What
if I am too broken to ever be fixed? How does one go about getting fixed?*

These questions and many more would torment my mind.
No one really knew what to say or do. Nothing made me feel better.
Going to church brought temporary comfort, but going meant
someone was missing, and coming home meant coming home
without him and all of his excitement and energy. Instead, joy seemed
illusive as my shattered heart ached for him. I still wanted a do-over!

*Okay, Lord, we did the right thing when we forgave those boys; we
know that. You did it through us, and we had no regrets, at least I know I
didn't. But, how do we go on? How do we put our family back together when
the one who made us a family is not here? Bill and I seemed to just be going
through the motions of life; neither of us could make things better.*

I vividly remember one night when Bill came home from

teaching. He came in the front door, and he just stood there looking at a small, woven basket filled with Will's broken toys. Up until this point, we had not moved anything of Will's in our home. Everything we touched just meant we had to say *good-bye* again and re-experience the pain of separation. The basket still sat in its place by the door because when it got full, Bill would take the basket of broken toys to his workshop every couple of months and hot glue, repair, or throw out the broken toys. He would then toss the restored toys into the toy box, which we affectionately called the *black hole*. As Bill silently stood still and focused on the basket of broken toys, I was unprepared for his next movement. He swiftly picked up the basket, and, with all his might, he hurled it into the wall of our living room. With heartbreaking sobbing, he fell to his knees and kept saying over and over, "I can't fix a damn thing. I can't fix a damn thing!"

I didn't go near him. I couldn't. I didn't have the energy. I couldn't even help myself and care for the baby, too. I felt the same despair and helplessness. I didn't have any extra to offer him. I couldn't let him pull me down into his abyss, could I? What would happen to Julie? I tried to be strong to resist the downward spiral we both seemed to be on. It was like being caught in a strong undertow and being swept out into a murky ocean and using every ounce of energy to save ourselves. Instead, I lifted Julie, now crying, and rocked her in her nursery until she went to sleep. I ran away into the familiar dark room in my mind and screamed at the top of my lungs. I blamed myself that night for not being good enough or strong enough. Bill was not the same after that; it was a new low. Darkness pervaded our home.

The elephant in the room was always with us, the subject that is too risky to bring up, yet it lurks behind every comment

Above the Overpass

THE CIRCUIT COURT OF SOUTH CAROLINA
ELEVENTH JUDICIAL CIRCUIT

HUBERT E. LONG
RESIDENT JUDGE
P.O. BOX 369
LEXINGTON. SOUTH CAROLINA 29072

TELEPHONE 359-8481

February 6, 1987

EDGEFIELD COUNTY
LEXINGTON COUNTY
McCORMICK COUNTY
SALUDA COUNTY

Mr. William Stapleton
6625 Dorechester Road, Lot 56
Charleston Heights, S. C. 29418

Dear Mr. Stapleton:

Enclosed please find a letter addressed to you but sent in care of my office. I had meant to write you earlier but have been in Court every day since the trial.

I want to take this opportunity to express to you how much it meant to me to hear your remarks at the end of the trial. Your remarks reinforced the other good things I had heard about you and your wife. I do not know what church you belong to, and in my opinion that is not important. The important thing to me about the trial as a whole was that you truly expressed Christian love by your words, as well as your acts, in a way that I have never experienced or witnessed before. Your witness not only was meaningful to me but to all who heard you or read about your faith. Your love witnesses more than one thousand sermons.

I wish for you and your wife the best of things in the future.

Very truly yours,

Hubert E. Long

HEL/jc

Enclosure

cc: Honorable Donnie V. Myers
    Honorable James Metts

We received this letter written after the trial by
the Honorable Hubert E. Long.

made. The subject that we wish had never happened. The subject we are both keenly aware of because of the deep regret, guilt, and shame inside that we both shared. The subject that was too painful to even voice, for fear of hurting the very person we wanted to protect. I am not referring to Will's death. I am talking about the life of our very first child -- the one we aborted before we married. There is truth to the statement that "you are as sick as your secrets." It was our *secret sin*, the one that we had made a pact to take with us to the grave. It was the elephant in the room that was too painful to face.

I was barely twenty at the time. Bill and I were crazy in love and engaged to be married. We went to New York City. New York, at the time, was the only state where abortion was legal. We had my pregnancy terminated.

With my strict religious upbringing, I had been so afraid of what my father and the church would think. I had never stopped blaming myself, even after all these years and with each miscarriage, I had carried the shame of having sex before we were married. And now I was wearing the blame and guilt for both of us. I had selfishly and cowardly murdered my unborn child many years prior because I was afraid of what others would think and speak. I believed the lie of the times that it was easier to *fix my problem* with an abortion than face the challenges of an unwanted pregnancy. I had been wearing guilt, shame, and now ALL the blame.

The '70s, were a time when the beginning of life was hotly debated, and the rhetoric of the day was that a baby was merely *tissue*. The church at large remained a sleeping, silent giant. I was the product of public schools where they taught that I had a right to my body. I never forgot the book we were required to read in high school health class, *Our Bodies, Ourselves*. It was full of the dogma and rhetoric of the day and quite opposite of what I had been reared to believe: Innately, I knew my body belonged to God. But I was caught up in the emotion of *romantic love*. I was so scared, and I read and reread that textbook, looking for a way to justify this was not the right time to have a baby. We had our whole lives ahead of us. Besides, I knew the sin I was guilty of was fornication (Yes, I even knew the Biblical word), sex outside of marriage. My conservative, Christian upbringing had made that point loud and clear. The shame and humiliation of my unborn child's legacy was unbearable in my naïve, narrow mind. I was so afraid of my parents and other people's disapproval that I broke my own moral code for *love* and purity and worse, I hurt the heart of God. Bill and I were married a few months later and pledged to God and each other that we would not knowingly sin against Him again. In fact, we would do all we could do to serve Him with our lives.

In the beginning of our marriage, not conceiving wasn't an issue; we enjoyed just being together. But as time went on and my pattern of miscarriages was established, I connected the losses to believe God was judging me. In my small, narrow, biased, twisted, human thinking, I was clearly being punished by God. "An eye for an eye" I religiously reasoned as I would go on to have a second miscarriage and then a third. The abortion represented my biggest regret in life, my depravity and loss of integrity. I felt like I was a disgrace to God and that this was my deserved punishment.

Time was moving forward, and the *church* was awakening to the pro-life issue. It was in our church that I saw a film of an unborn baby in the womb for the first time. I only felt more condemned and more ashamed. Everyone around me seemed angry and outraged. Church was certainly not a safe place for me to confess something so horrible. I pronounced myself guilty every day and lost all self-respect and self-worth. In fact, as the church awakened, I tumbled even further into the pit of self-condemnation and became stuck in guilt and shame. I would, from then on, see myself as a worthless, selfish murderer. Would God never consider the score to be settled because I took a life? Believing that I had done the unforgivable, I sentenced myself to life in the prison of barrenness! We would serve God but never feel like it was enough.

Then, still with distorted and twisted reasoning, we would amazingly conceive Will in our tenth year of marriage. It was only then that I would begin to finally feel forgiven and released from guilt, but I could not shake off the deeply rooted shame; by then it had become part of the fabric of my soul. No matter how much good I would do, I would never feel good enough for God. I would always feel condemned.

Now, with Will's death, I was questioning God again after these many years. I believed then after three miscarriages that Will's birth had been God's forgiveness of me and that in some way the score was now even. It was not until I held Will in my arms and cared for him day after day that my self-condemnation would begin to melt. I knew that God could have prevented Will's death, so the harsh reality was that HE had allowed it! What more did God want? Was I not forgiven? Did I deserve this? Did we bring this tragedy upon ourselves? I would begin a downward spiral of sorrow and depression. I wallowed in confusion and hopeless heartache as I wore the *Scarlet Letter* on my soul.

Who is this God that my parents taught me to believe in? Who is this

God of the Bible? Who is the Creator of life? What does He want from me? Is this higher perverted manipulative justice an eye for an eye or punishment so that I will obey more perfectly?

I was more afraid of Him than in love with Him. If I ever needed to hear from God, it was then. Is that why HE arranged my trip to Heaven? Is that why He gave me that *vision*? And what about my dumb question about the bride? Yes, even amid all the questions, self-condemnation, and shame, I knew that God had not left me. Amazingly, even though I believed I was the worst of sinners, I believed in my mind that HE was BIG enough to love me even though I felt so unlovable. At the same time, I also believed that He was trying to teach me something by punishing me. I could hear harsh voices from my childhood, ending with "You made your bed, now lie in it!"

After all, God seemed to be going way out of His way to get my attention; first, by taking me to see Heaven, and then the *vision* the night Will was killed. Obviously, He needed for me to learn something in all this inner turmoil. One thing I was certain of: I will never forget the strength of His voice when He assured me that "He was BIGGER and to remember Job." It was a quest of sorts, a quest in the midst of a spiritual battle for our very lives.

I read and reread the first chapter of Job. It slowly began to make sense to me through the Holy Spirit. In the face of our tragic grief and through the vision in the ER that night, God had made it clear that HE was in control; He was even bigger than Satan and his evil in these circumstances. In God's *BIGNESS*, He had reached down to comfort me on the darkest night of my life -- that night on the highway and in the emergency room. I sometimes wondered why God went to the trouble to take me to Heaven yet not warn me of Will's death.

I am at peace now, knowing that if I had known ahead of time, it would have only birthed fear in my soul, and one cannot have faith where fear exists. Instead, He gave me increased faith in the life to come, and I now have an incredible and supernatural insider's view of where Will is living and growing up, a most spectacularly industriously brilliant place of peace and joy, light and love.

I would spend much time reading and rereading the book of Job. In this Hebrew story in the Old Testament of the Bible, a good and wealthy man named Job was diligent in caring for his family and turned away from doing evil. It is a dramatic story of how Job, even in his weakness and secret fears, walked and talked with God. He was known by all the people in his region for his integrity and righteousness. Then his life takes a horrific turn when he unknowingly gets caught up in a battle ground between God and Satan, symbolizing good and evil. With no warning, and seemingly out of nowhere, he loses everything he has: sheep, cattle, servants, his ten children, and finally his health. It is a heartbreaking, yet inspiring story of the character, integrity, patience, and endurance of an amazing man of faith, as he poetically reasons with friends and God as to why this calamity has come upon him. He is referred to often when we use the expression: *The patience of Job.* Even as Job endured the tragic losses, he could have never known that one day his trials would be a source of comfort for others, including myself, who could feel his heartache and marvel at the depth of his faith through the aftermath.

*"After Job heard all those reports, he got up and
tore his robe. He shaved his head. Then he fell to
the ground And worshiped the Lord. He said, 'I
was born naked, and I'll leave here naked. You
have given, and you have taken away. May your
name be praised.'"* (Job 1: 20, NIRV)

The most fascinating part of the story unfolded for me as
I became intrigued with the back story that gave me insight into
the war betwe Good (GOD) and Evil (SATAN) as it continues in
the spiritual realm (Job 1: 6-22, NIRV).

*"One day angels came to the Lord. Satan
also came with them. The Lord said to Satan,
'Where have you come from?' Satan answered,
'From traveling all around the earth. I've been
going from one end of it to the other.' Then the
Lord said to Satan, 'Have you thought about
my servant Job? There isn't anyone on earth like
him. He is honest. He does what is right. He has
respect for me and avoids evil.'"* (Job 1: 6-8,
NIRV)

I must admit that I initially missed the significance of
God's first question. Not only did God start the conversation,
but it also explains why the verse "he (Satan) roams around like
a roaring lion seeking those to devour" that kept going over
and over in my mind the night Will was killed. This confirmed
to me that this was a spiritual battle. Even on the highway that

night, God wanted me to know that He was there the whole time, and then, HE shines the spotlight on Job! As I pondered this, I couldn't help but think, *Are You trying to tell me Lord, that it was because Job was honest, good, respectful of You, and trying to do right that You pointed at him to be tested by the adversary? Geez, thanks God, way to go God…you couldn't leave well enough alone? Wow! I had just never seen the fact that it was Job's goodness and trust in God that would reveal that God already knew Job would be faithful to Him through it all.*

"*In spite of everything, Job didn't sin by blaming God for doing anything wrong*" (1 Job: 22, NIRV). Bill and I were far from being Job, but apparently God knew us better than we knew ourselves because He truly used us to forgive murderers, and we had proven faithful. Now, if we could only find a way to forgive ourselves. I was angry. I didn't like it. I didn't like it that God could point His big finger and single out whomever He wanted. I didn't like the fact that He had ALL the power. I didn't like it that God had the power to lift a *hedge of protection* to prove a point to Satan, even though God did put limits on Satan's power.

First, he was told he could touch his possessions but not Job's life, and secondly, he could touch Job's body but not take Job's life. I wasn't comforted by knowing that God could do whatever He wanted to do, when and however HE wanted to do it. I resisted this with every fiber in my being. After all, in my heart I was scared. I was still the hurting victim unable and unwilling to see myself clearly, a person who would in my mind never be good enough. I had so much to learn about the Sovereignty of God and His love. But in my need, I would desperately hold on to the comfort that Job's words brought through the verses, "For when I am tried and purified, I shall come forth as gold" (Hamilton). And "*though He slay me, yet I will hope in Him*" (Job 13:15, ESV).

If Job could do it, I could do it, or die trying. The wound was still too raw. Who did God think HE was anyway? Even the thought that we may be pawns of some *cosmic power game* that God and Satan might play drove me running to that small dark room in my head, where the heartbroken and fragile little girl would stand and scream as loud as she could.

XII

God's Patience

"Patience is more than endurance. A saint's life is in the hands of God like a bow and arrow in the hands of an archer. God is aiming at something the saint cannot see, and HE stretches and strains, and every now and again the saint says, 'I cannot stand anymore.' God does not heed, HE goes on stretching till HIS purpose is in sight, then HE lets fly. Trust yourself in God's hands. For what have you need of patience just now. Maintain your relationship to Jesus Christ by the patience of faith. Though HE slays me, yet will I wait for HIM."

Oswald Chambers

Being a mother has been the most purposeful role I have ever filled. It is a role that God has used to show me His amazing love for me as His own child. It has brought me a greater understanding of His love and patience for me.

One morning, the sun was shining, so Will and I were at the neighborhood park with all the other Moms and their children. I was a little older than most of them. It had taken eleven years and three miscarriages for my husband and I to conceive our little boy. Will Jr. was an active, healthy, eighteen-month-old toddler, and I was still settling into the reality of all the energy, effort and responsibility it took to raise a child. I looked at the other younger mothers who all seemed so relaxed. How did they do it? I sat and chatted with the girl on the bench beside me and tried to relax, too.

Will was happily playing in the sandbox by the lake fence. A cute little girl about three-years-old with blonde ponytails, complete with ribbons and bows, was playing in the sandbox alongside of Will. With no reason and before anyone could stop her, she stood up and poured her full bucket of sand right on top of Will's head! I leapt up as Will began to wail and rub his eyes. I scooped him up into my arms to try and keep him from making it even worse. In a moment it was a tragic day at the park!

I did the best I could to flush Will's eyes with bottled water and battle with his flailing arms to keep him from rubbing the sand further into his eyes. During trying to calm him, and hurriedly gathering our belongings, I found myself feeling something else rising deep inside of me that I had never felt before. It was growing more intense by the moment. It was raw and it was primitive. It was an internal rage that began rising, a gut felt, primal emotion that made me feel animalistic, like a lioness. I realized for the first time in my life that I could maim or kill to protect my child! The intensity of this seeming irrational depth of rage was real. I sincerely wanted to hurl that little girl over the fence into the lake nearby and walk away!

As I fastened Will in his stroller though, I became acutely aware of all the eyes on us. I guess they were waiting for me to outwardly react, but I just mumbled something about naptime and time to go home. The truth is, I had to recover and pull myself together. I was shocked at my own emotions. I realized, of course, that it was the immenseness of the love I felt for this little boy fully accompanied by a desire to do anything it took to protect him. After our naps, self-control and ice cream redeemed that day.

Many times, I would be reminded of that day after the murder trial. In fact, almost every time when I thought of our supernatural ability to forgive the boys it was with the realization that He did that through us because He was in us through the Holy Spirit. God used Bill and me, and it was the right thing to do, and yet, we struggled to forgive ourselves and each other. I felt victimized by evil. Would this be the story of the rest of my life? What was this thing called forgiveness? I did not want to be bitter. I would have so much more to learn about the depths of God's love and patience with His children. I would listen to the voice of the accuser and believe the rhetoric of the enemy as he would tell me it was my entire fault and that if I had not had the abortion, this would not have happened to Will. In my pain and self-condemnation, I was missing the most important message -- that God had entrusted Job with these challenges. God knew Job best because He created Job. I would certainly try to identify with Job. God knew Job's heart, and HE knew he wouldn't curse HIM. God knew Job better than he knew himself! God saw Job from the only true perspective; God loved him, and Job belonged to Him. Job wasn't a god. Job was an imperfect man, a fearful, flawed human, doing the best he could out of his love for God. HE loved God, and God knew it. I had such a low, unhealthy, and distorted view of myself because of my failures and shortcomings. After all, I was a believer; there was a higher standard set for me. I had no concept of what grace meant at that time. I only knew criticism, judgment, guilt, and shame at the time, most of it coming from within myself and through the insidious voice of the accuser in my mind. I could not even begin to receive God's unconditional forgiveness, acceptance, and love for me. Even though God's voice had told me to "Remember Job," I could not align myself with Job. Instead, I was caught up in my own darkness. Job was so much better than me. I was tormented in my mind every day. It would take more time for me. I did know and believe that HE had not left me, but He was allowing me to marinate in my tortured sorrow.

God had allowed, not caused, the events in Job's life, just as he had allowed the tragedy in our lives. It was not the suffering that troubled us; it was the depth of the pain of undeserved anguish and suffering. It seemed so harsh and unjust. I had always tried so hard to do the right things, the right way, and then we were blindsided by this and knocked down. I would have done penance of any sort to make things right with God, but to take our child back seemed unusually cruel! I had even torturously wondered in my "eye for an eye, tooth for a tooth" mentality whether all women who had abortions had children who died.

At one point of despair, I was thinking about researching how many women who lost a child had undergone abortion. People who feel condemned often judge others. I was so wrongly convinced this was *God's justice*, and, instead, it was my twisted, human attempt to make senseless events make sense. I had often thought that I would like to do the research on that point. Would it prove God's anger or His love? Could something that felt like anger be God's love? Even as I write this I am amazed at His great patience and love for me. I was on a personal quest, a quest to really know, once and for all, who God is.

I know with all my heart God did want me to see Him clearly. Somehow, through my upbringing, I believed that God was safe. We want to teach our children truth, but somehow, we have no way of knowing they truly understand that He is a God who isn't always a safe God, but who is always a good God.

We live in a world where fear abounds. We love our children, so we do all we can to keep our children safe from the time they come home from the hospital with rear-facing car seats to seat belts, helmets for their bikes, and locks on all our cabinets. The list is endless of our efforts to protect our children. The truth though is quite frankly this: no matter how noble our efforts, we set ourselves up when we think that all our efforts will work. C.S. Lewis understood this fully when he wrote the classic, *The Lion the Witch and the Wardrobe*.

God would reveal this truth to me one day as I read about when the children prepare to go to see Aslan, who is the type of Christ. They ask Mr. Beaver, "Is Aslan safe?" And he replies, "No, but HE is always good." This statement is so simple yet profound because the truth of knowing and understanding a Sovereign God simply means that HE can do whatever HE wants to do, whenever HE wants to do it, however HE needs to get it done, and with whomever HE needs to allow it to happen to! HE is still BIGGER!

People around me have sayings that state, "They're all good people" or "They have a good heart." I am sure those making these statements mean well, but nothing could be farther from the truth. God says, "The heart of man is deceitfully wicked." Even as a parent, I can tell you that like me, one never has to teach her children to do something wrong. In fact, loving parents wear themselves out trying to teach children to do right. We all come into the fallen world programmed to do wrong if left on our own. If we don't take the time to teach our children to do right, we neglect their character development. It's the reason children need parents who consistently teach and model right living. Goodness is caught in a home where it is valued, and imperfection is expected and covered with grace and forgiveness.

There is no person who is always good. Only God is always good. That is why God had to send His only perfect Son to pave the way back to Him. His flawless Son was the only perfect One able to wear our sin and die for our world. God wants us to make the connection between the wrong we commit and the One who paid it all. The pain we were experiencing was sharing in the pain He felt for us. We were connected forever through pain and sorrow.

God was stretching Bill and me His way. He so wanted us to see him as BIGGER, as being able to fully comfort us in our grief, as being able to enlarge our lives through this tragedy, so we could be used to comfort others. He clearly hadn't caused the tragedy, but He allowed it to happen in a world where tragedies happen -- a fallen, broken world. He was there that night on I-26 to receive Will's soul back to Himself and able to use this evil for good as He promises to do for all who love Him (Romans 8:28). My perspective was beginning to change to God's at this point, and I was beginning to embrace the deeper truths of God's Word instead of being offended.

He wanted us to see that no matter how good we try to be, we can never achieve His perfection. We could never have protected Will from this! God's sovereign perspective is far beyond what we can see, and only He knows the good He is doing through the circumstance even when we don't. It is always about doing one's best and finishing well, like Job, who had strength of character with his integrity, patience, and endurance to never, never, never give up.

I wish I could say that we caught the truth soon after

Will's death, but instead we remained stuck in the mire, focused on ourselves, on our loss, on our hurt and pain. We were unable to reconcile our guilt for our past sins. We felt like it was our entire fault that, somehow, we had the power to bring tragedy onto ourselves. We still did not get the fact that we could not play God! As human beings, we don't have that much power, but at the time, sadly we were ensnared in that lie from Satan. We were being held captive by a lie. We wrongly thought we were being punished and that God was getting even for our disobedience many years before. We would have a lot more to learn about God's grace and His patience before we could heal and be free.

We were so wrong. We were like two inmates sitting in a jail cell with the keys to our cell in our hands and not using the pass key of grace. At the time, we were so broken; we could not understand what God wanted to do in and through us. And in His great mercy and love, he continued to work with us and bring us to a place of healing and a clearer understanding of this great tragedy. I would come to realize that one can never get rid of pain and suffering in this world, and one can't get rid of problems by getting rid of God. I wanted to have more of God's perspective on the world. I wanted to see my life through His eyes. That became my continued personal quest.

It was shortly after the *breakdown* when Bill had collapsed in the living room that he announced to me that he had decided to move our mobile home, which we were currently living in, up to the property in North Carolina. Since we already owned it, we should move it up on the mountain to be nearer Will. That way, we would feel closer to him. This news did not appeal to me at all, even though I was looking forward to living up there in a few years. At this point, my emotional, mental, and physical energy were knocking on empty as I climbed into bed each night. Bill seemed determined that this was what God was directing him to do. I was not on board with the timing of it all.

There is an idiom that says *hindsight is 20/20*. As I look back on this frame of time, it is easy to see that we both had classic symptoms of PTSD - Post Traumatic Stress Disorder, but in 1987, no one ever talked about it or knew about it.

Here are some of the symptoms of PTSD:

- Anger, Irritability
- Depression, Hopelessness

- Guilt, Shame, Self-blame
- Suicidal Thoughts /Feelings

- Substance Abuse
- Feeling Alienated/Alone

- Feelings of Mistrust/Betrayal
- Physical Aches /Pains

We had all the symptoms, except substance abuse. There seemed to be no reasoning with Bill once he made up his mind. He would not listen to sound advice that recommended that one not make any moves the first year after a death or significant loss. He was determined to move us, and I didn't have the emotional energy to stop him. Instead, I told him that he would have to do it all, and I just wouldn't fight him.

It had taken a couple of years for me to get used to the idea of moving south from New Jersey. I had always admired people who could just pick up and go and do spontaneous things, but it was not in my hard wiring. Now, with losing Will and moving, it meant uprooting again. It meant more loss of my church and my friends, and we were still far away from family. I wasn't ready to start over in a new place. I wanted to heal first! We were so broken! What about Julie? She deserved healthy parents, and at this time, we couldn't even help each other. I made my heartfelt appeal to Bill hoping he would understand the emotional, physical, and even financial drain this would be, but he would not wait. He wanted a *fresh start*. I just wanted to be still. I didn't have the energy to argue any more.

I told him, "I will care for Julie, and I will pack up the things in the house. Will's room, however, must stay the same. You will have to do everything else to get us there." At the time, my memory went back to the trip to Heaven and the Messenger's words: "Follow your husband." "Okay, Lord, I can trust You, and I will."

Bill would start his piano tuning business over from scratch. He would continue to develop the land into a home site, and I would blindly follow. My biggest effort was trying to be the best mom I could be for Julie. Healing from our trauma would be difficult under the best of circumstances, but Bill was persistent and capable of making this move to the mountains, so we were relocated by that spring of 1987.

We were strangers in a strange land. I felt like a spectator, sitting on a bleacher, watching the game, but having no enthusiasm to be there. We had a hard time healing over the year ahead. Will had only been gone six months. We were so broken. We ran into challenge after challenge with the land. We had moved precipitously. Bill seemed tireless; he had to keep moving.

Instead of working through our grief, we were developing seventeen acres of land. There was so much time, money, and paperwork involved, daunting for any young couple, and we were

Will and Bill, father and son, loved to climb trees and have fun together. This is one such moment. (This picture was still in the camera when the crime happened.)

Top: A happy time. It's summer 1986, and Julie Lin is born and joins big brother, Will, who is almost four-years- old. Bottom: Will playing hide-n-seek.

Will died November 5, 1986. Will's headstone, was placed on the spot where he and Daddy would sit and count the railroad cars. Below: Daddy (Bill) and Julie Lin visiting Will's grave.

already knocking on empty. We had trouble getting power run to it because we needed underground lines run. This involved the railroad and regulations. Then, drilling a well only revealed that we were better off capping a spring, which Bill did at double the expense. In addition, we were forced to have a boundary line moved, which required us to develop two home sites at increasing costs and stress. I won't go on and on with the details, but I'll say that most of that season is a blur because I was *checked out.* I was absolutely no use to anyone but Julie. My song in that season of life became the theme song from an old sitcom called *Green Acres.* "You are my wife, good-bye -city life!"

I still laugh out of sheer relief that we survived, especially when I remember the telephone, believe it or not. At one point, we did have our phone installed on a telephone pole, just not at the top though, thank God! No kidding! These are the many reasons I counsel those experiencing loss **not** to make any major changes the first year.

I often look back on that time in our lives and marvel at the human goodness and compassion of people. Ultimately, I knew it was the love of a powerful God that was taking care of us. But it was also a very humbling time. We had always been so independent, and now there were things that we just could not do on our own. That year we lived as displaced persons, at times desperate to depend on the kindness and hospitality of our new friends in the Cove. We were humbled to receive. We were learning that being on the receiving end is much harder than giving because it assaults one's pride. Two amazing families took us in and let us live with them for a few months at a time when Bill was working on our land. Each family was generous and unique, as they willingly shared not only their roofs but their lives with us. More astonishingly, people were added to the gratitude list in my heart, knowing all the while that it would be impossible for us to ever repay their kindness. The memories still humble me knowing there is no way to repay such kindness and compassion. I can only pay it forward.

For me, the tragedy was like the first violent pass of a harsh storm or tornado over a city, knocking down everything in its path. Now, left with debris to clear and with stubborn roots still exposed in the ground, I still was not ready to replant anything. I felt like a damaged remnant. I felt depleted and ravaged by the storm. I did not know what I had left in me. I had always resisted change. I would read and ask God to give me what I needed. I needed to know and to understand so that I could heal. I had so much confusion. I felt like I would never feel alive again.

On one of my parents' visits to our home, my mother handed me a book from someone in her church. They had told her that God had placed me on their heart and wanted me to have the book. It was called *The Transformation of the Inner Man* by John and Paula Sanford. It was an exhaustive, in-depth analysis of how God designed us. I was instantly intrigued, but it was not a quick read. It would take a good part of the next year and then some to grasp the depth of what the authors were saying. It was a big beginning step in my quest to figure God out. I laugh even now to myself of my arrogance at the time in even remotely thinking that I *could* figure HIM out. What the book really helped me do was help me find out who I really was and His purpose for my life.

Developing a homestead was unsettling to say the least. Bill threw himself into the back-breaking work, and Julie was curious and crawling around everywhere. In a few months, we settled in, and I will forever remember the joy of having running water finally coming through our pipes! There were many times back then when I would just let the water run and thank God for it flowing through our spigots. Will had been gone for one year now, and we were just getting established in our home. We had hopes to try to assimilate into the new *mountain culture* this coming year.

Bill's talent was his calling card. All he had to do was sit down at a piano and start to play; he could make it sing, so before long, we were invited to many churches to share our music and our testimony of forgiveness. Talking about Will and bringing the hope of eternal life and salvation brought meaning and purpose to our lives. Every time I was able to relate our story, I could tell He was comforting and healing me, too. God was making a way for my healing.

It wasn't long before Bill was invited to perform with the local Community Theatre. He played and wrote and arranged a lot of the music for the production. He put his whole heart into it. Music was always the best therapy for him. I got involved a little bit, too, with singing. It introduced us to a lot of the local people, and we began to live life again even though on the inside and never far from the surface, I still ached, missing Will. It was a new life, a new town, new friends, and even from the outside, we looked like a new family with a baby. Will and his life were disappearing, but I was desperate to remember. I cataloged pictures, wrote down memories, and read my Bible a lot. I was still on a quest to find answers to my questions about God and this life that I was reluctantly living.

Those first few years after Will's tragic death were sad, hard, and lonely for me. Every time I looked at Julie, I would sense Will's missing presence. It was always missing. Those early months of her life, Will had been her constant attendant as he watched over her. He had appointed himself as her protector. One day, he came to tell me after Julie had been crying that he had *fixed* the baby! I quickly ran to see what he meant, and he had placed her thumb in her mouth (right thumb - just like he did) and it worked! She was then vigorously sucking on her own thumb. I remember hugging him and telling him what a kind and helpful big brother he was already. I thought it was very interesting that soon after Will was no longer here for her, she asserted her own individuality by switching over to her left index finger to suck on. It was a constant and gentle reminder to me that she had learned from a loving teacher, but she was still her own person. Many times, I felt challenged to find a way not to let my heartache cloud her bright little life.

Julie was light and sunshine wherever she was! She loved people and never knew a stranger. She would draw people to her with her *cuteness*. She was bright, playful, and curious -- everything I needed. These moments would make me smile and laugh again. But I couldn't overcome the deep sadness, the longing to be near Will; he should be here with us. I felt judged and shamed by God. I can attest that the heaviest burden you'll ever carry is the burden of guilt and shame. Bill and I were not doing well. I still felt that he blamed me. I blamed myself even more, but we didn't talk about it. We lived like roommates. We shared a roof, played with the baby, but had no sharing of the heaviness in our hearts. I still cried a lot. Many days were spent up by Will's grave at the entrance to our land. Julie would run around and play, and I would make daisy chains for her to wear in her hair, but my thoughts were far away.

I was overwhelmed with life, many times fantasizing about how to end it. I didn't really want to live. Real life was just too hard, but I couldn't face leaving my sweet Julie either. Her youthful exuberance helped to plant me in the moment, even though I felt alone, and I missed my family so much. I didn't feel like I fit in anywhere.

XIII

God's Perfection

"For You created my inmost being; you knit me together in my mother's womb. I praise You because I am fearfully and wonderfully made. Your works are wonderful, I know that full well."

Psalm 139:13-14 (NIV)

Bill and I were more distanced than we had ever been. I didn't have the energy to pretend anymore. I guess one might say that became our new normal. Our new friends and neighbors were all wonderful, compassionate people. We would get invitations to come to all kinds of churches and present our worship music and give a testimony and message of what God had done during the murder of our son, and each time I felt like God was using those times to gently heal us. We couldn't really talk about it to each other, but we could share it with others. I know it was the Holy Spirit and His comfort that was keeping us moving.

Bill questioned God a lot and began experimenting with another denomination; he even had invited them into our home to meet every week. I was irritated with the twisting of scripture and Bill's inability to *catch* much of their error, but it reawakened the teacher/learner part of me, and I found myself pouring over the scriptures to defend my core foundational beliefs. It also made me more empathetic toward Bill because he had not had the scriptures woven into the fabric of his childhood as I had.

Looking back, I believe that God used that time for me to clearly define what was really important for me to believe about Him. I remember with every *debate* clearly hearing my dad's voice saying, "If you don't stand for something, you'll fall for anything!" My strength began to be renewed, but I felt like I was fighting for my faith.

In contrast, it was frightening to see Bill begin to drift away from the foundational principles of our faith when I, on the other hand, was growing stronger than I had ever been defending it. One day, he insisted we go to one of their meetings. I complied, but as we drove up the mountain, we were able to finally have a heartfelt talk. We went that once out of courtesy to the ones who had come to our home, but we never went back, and they never returned to our home.

I was also reading everything I could about inner healing and listening to the Christian radio out of Black Mountain, North Carolina, every day. I would have a radio going in most of the rooms in the house so that all through the day I could hear from teachers and preachers, such as Dr. James Dobson, Chuck Swindoll, and Elizabeth Elliott as I went about my day with Julie. I was learning who I was in Christ. The voice in my head that was telling me I was worthless, bad, and stupid was becoming more like a whisper as God's voice would overpower it and tell me I was fearfully and wonderfully made, and I was beginning to believe it! It seemed like everything I was listening to had spiritual medicine to heal my fractured inner spirit.

Our music teaching and tuning business was reestablished now, and life was settling down. Julie was so smart and growing beautifully even though she didn't walk until she was fourteen months old. It was a strange thing that she seemed to have no desire to walk. She simply loved being held, and we held her a lot. She did begin to walk though, and we noticed that she walked on her toes a lot and was very graceful in her movements. Bill and I both agreed that as soon as she was old enough, she should start dance lessons. We called her our little *wood-sprite*. She began taking dance at age three and loved every minute. She was my constant companion along with her imaginary friend, *Gillie*. By the time she was turning four, I had decided I was going to home school her.

It was at the kitchen table one day when we had switched seats and were going over a simple little workbook. She told me, "Mom, you need to talk louder so that I can hear you better." Pointing to her right ear she said, "This one is broke."

Puzzled, I began asking questions. "When was the last time you were able to hear?" Then I started to name sometimes in recent past events. "Did your ear work in Sunday school this week?"

"No."

"Did you hear when you were playing with Jenny?"

"No."

"Did you hear when you were in New Jersey at the beach this summer with Granma and Pop Pop?"

"No."

As I led her through events back in time, I would quickly come to realize Julie was telling me she had never, ever heard a sound in her right ear. Bill and I were stunned to realize we had not picked up on this. But it also grimly reminded Bill that he had also experienced temporary hearing loss the night of Will's death.

The next day, I took her to see our pediatrician, and she administered a hearing test. I will never forget the stunned and colorless look on our doctor's face as she came out of the testing room. She had been seeing Julie for most of her young life and had never suspected. We were referred to an audiologist and all was confirmed. The injury apparently occurred during the explosion of the impact as the boulder ripped through the car. All the little hairs inside the cochlea of Julie's right ear were sheared off during that tragic night, rendering her profoundly deaf in her right ear. The hearing in her left ear appeared normal. We were devastated for her. It was one more remnant of the destruction; however, Julie didn't seem fazed. She had never known anything else.

But now, the decision to home school was essential. Up until this point of time, Julie's diction was perfect. Now that we knew she would never hear her dance music in stereo and / or be able to tell sound direction, we believed that the best-case scenario for Julie was learning in a quiet atmosphere. The audiologist agreed one-on-one instruction would be the best route for these early days of learning. When one has difficulty hearing, it is very difficult to differentiate sounds with background noise. I found it surprising that there was no option to have corrective surgery or hearing aids, but in Julie's case, none of that was viable. The doctors said it would only frustrate her. It was difficult to fully understand that we did not have a way to fix her hearing. Even when cochlear implants came to be, Julie was not a candidate for them because they are only for profound hearing loss in both ears.

Homeschooling Julie was the best solution for her, and she was already ahead of the learning curve. Julie was such a social child, and I knew she really wanted to be in school with the other kids, especially her best friend, Jenny. I felt myself slipping back onto the pity-pot, bitterness welling up inside that she was irreparably damaged. But I was getting better at taking my thoughts captive and trusting Him as I was feeling stronger emotionally. I have peace knowing that what we did was the best thing for Julie at the time. Most hearing-impaired adults with Julie's limitations have a deaf accent, but to speak with her today, one would never guess she was hearing impaired. Also, as an interesting side note, it is amusing to know that even though she was born and raised in the South, she actually has more of a Northeastern accent like her dad and me.

Over the years since Will's death, we had been asked by several close and well-meaning friends whether we were trying to have another child. My quick answer was always, "No. It hurts too much to lose one." Bill and I weren't trying to have another child, but we weren't trying not to have one either. I was in my late thirties and because of my previous history of difficult deliveries, I wasn't expecting to have any more children. Then, on the heels of the discovery of Julie's hearing loss, I realized I was pregnant.

Initially, I was shocked; maybe it was a menopause issue. I purposely did not tell Bill right away. I needed to process this in my own mind. Even though it had been almost five years, I knew Bill and I were not recovered from the trauma of Will's death, but I also knew that God was Bigger and that children were His greatest gift. Selfishly, I nurtured the thought of the beautiful little life, a masterpiece forming in God's secret place within me. How amazing of God! But in my dark quiet times, I was afraid, too. What if I also lost this one? Will You let me keep another precious child, Lord? Will this be our reconciliation -- Yours and mine? I was also fearful of Bill's response; he seemed so volatile these days.

He needed to know, but I wanted to plan a special time to

tell him. Instead, he would discover the news as we were going into Asheville the next weekend. The winding mountain road we took made me so nauseous that we needed to pull over. He quickly figured it out, and I discovered I had no reason to fear. He was so very happy! I thought that maybe now we might find **us** again. Julie was happy just to see us happy and began looking forward to being a big sister, often practicing with her cabbage patch doll baby.

Through the pregnancy, I struggled with crippling fear of losing this baby. I seemed to be fighting my thoughts continually, but I was standing on His promises in the Word, and during that time, God was so comforting and real to me as He met me in my uncertainty and questioning. I held tight to Psalm 139 where God talks about how we are *"fearfully and wonderfully made,"* and how *"He knows every single day to come into our lives."* I found comfort in knowing that before Will was born, God knew Will would only live with us three years and eleven months. I was overwhelmed with gratefulness for having him that long. Reminding myself again, that I had seen the children playing in Heaven and knew that Will would not want to come back.

I had always been fascinated with midwifery, especially since we had birthed Will and Julie in a birth center. I loved the holistic approach to childbirth instead of the over managed medical view. I reasoned that because women had been giving birth since the beginning of time, it was a natural function of a woman's body and not a medical issue, unless health complications arose. Because we lived in the mountains, I only had to ask my pediatrician to refer me to a midwife. We chose to have a home birth.

Our doctor was an experienced doctor who had birthed

her own children at home. She partnered with a delightful and seasoned midwife, who had delivered hundreds of babies up in the mountains. Everyone was fully aware of the risks, and even with my history of hemorrhaging after both Will's and Julie's births, they were confident that I could have a home birth, so I was organized and ready ahead of time.

My parents had just arrived in their motor home to celebrate Julie's fifth birthday. Julie had been eagerly looking forward to Granma and Pop Pop's visit, and she was already begging to sleep that night in the motor home with them. Even with the best of plans, there is always a variable, so with a month still to go in my pregnancy, I began mild labor pains that night. At first, we thought it was Braxton Hicks contractions or excitement of Granma and Pop Pop's arrival. I was a bit anxious, and their presence and care for Julie seemed like perfect timing.

It was 1991 before ultrasounds were routine for pregnancies. After careful examinations by both the doctor and the midwife, they both concluded that there were two separate heartbeats and upon examination, they were sure they felt little toes and a head at the same place. They concurred that there were two babies coming. We were so happy at the thought of twins but overwhelmed at the same time! It appeared that I was in the beginning stages of labor. My pregnancy had been uneventful, so even with the early labor and anticipation of twins, we all agreed to move forward with a home birth. The doctor and midwife scrambled to get duplicate supplies and emergency medical equipment in place, just in case. The contractions were coming regularly for a few hours, but even after all the poking and prodding, my labor completely stopped. They told me to go to bed, and they would stay nearby, which meant they would be trying to catch forty winks as they were draped over the living room furniture with one eye open, thinking the babies may come quickly during the night.

If it is possible to stop labor with unmitigated fear, then I did it. I was so scared and perplexed, I just couldn't seem to settle myself, so in the wee hours of the morning with the dawn coming soon, I quietly left the house through the back door. I decided to walk down our moon-lit driveway and then walk up the knoll to Will's grave. By the time I reached his grave, I collapsed in sheer exhaustion. I knew I could not bear another child's death. I was having such a difficult time facing down my fears! It was just like the evil one to be tormenting and accusing me when I felt so weak. *Oh God! Please take away my fear!* I realized, maybe for the first time, in a fresh wave of anguish, how angry I still was with God but yet afraid at the same time to admit it to Him. I guess I had been afraid He would strike me dead on the spot! Yet, it was in that moment that I screamed at God. I yelled at Him and told Him how angry I was.

"Where were your angels? One little tip of an angel's wing and the boulder would not have hit the car! You were supposed to keep us safe! I hate you for having Will when I don't! You are cruel to give and then take!"

I sobbed as I lay on top of Will's grave and begged God to take away my fears, sadness, and tears. I was so tired of the crying and sadness. Then, exhausted and spent by my tantrum, I laid there sobbing, too weak to stand. Contractions were starting up again. I tried to gather what strength I could, so I could get on my feet. As I struggled to regain my balance on that still and muggy July morning, a strong cool breeze came out of nowhere. It blew into my wet, tearstained face.

As it dried my tears instantly, I heard God's voice audibly say, "You are mine, my daughter. I made you. I know everything about you." And then with a gentle chuckle in His voice, He said, "You can be angry, my child, because My love for you is stronger. I am with you, and I promise I will dry every tear from your eyes."

I was immediately infused with strength and comforted to hear from Him. The labor pains started back up as I waddled back up the road to the house. God and I finally totally reconciled that day on Will's hill. I was purged of my anger and fear at last! I wanted that conversation to mean I would never cry again, but instead, it has proved true through the years -- the fact that He still faithfully dries every tear I cry.

By the time I arrived back at the house, I was informed that more help was on the way, and two more nurse midwives were coming. Everything was abuzz; there was so much activity, and I just wanted it over! Bill was already stressed out. This *simple home birth* was getting more complicated by the minute. He was already agitated by all the extra people involved.

No labor is easy; I steadily but slowly progressed. I believed with all my soul that God was going to give us another son. We didn't even have a girl's name picked out. All I was sure of was that I did not want to live anymore if a baby was going to die. I had to have the strength to trust God. The labor was my worst. I wanted to rip out the IV hanging from the curtain rod because it hurt so badly in my hand. When I couldn't stand any more. . . . The midwife announced, "It's a boy!"

I could feel myself slipping away. Before I lost consciousness, I remember locking eyes with a beautiful little boy whose eyes were bright and alert but who wasn't breathing. That was the moment in time that God gave me to always remember. Benjamin took one look at his mommy and our eyes locked. He reached into my heart and gripped my soul forever. A yell for oxygen for the baby, and then, "We're losing her . . . ."

It had been almost two days since giving birth to our son when I fully awoke. The midwives had tended to me and the baby around the clock, even starting the baby to nurse. I asked about the other baby, but my midwife said not to worry; there had been just one baby. She had only shared that I had lost too much blood and needed to rest and not worry. I could tell she was reticent to tell me more just then, but as soon as I was stronger, I pressed her, and she admitted that she had been just as puzzled by all the signs of twins I had exhibited. In fact, she had been so perplexed that she went to see the granny midwife who trained her. My midwife relayed to her all the symptoms and indications of my pregnancy, and the granny midwife seemed to know immediately what it was.

She told her, "You have experienced an *angel baby*." She explained that in her many years of experience, it was a phenomenon that happens when the mother might die. She went on to explain that in the few times she had experienced it, the manifestation of the *angel baby* ensured that more help would be there to save the mother's life. Now, my midwife would confirm that.

Through the next week, I was regaining strength, not only physically, but spiritually and emotionally. Having my parents nearby to care for us was healing. The midwives had said that my dad had been the team leader with prayer and even they felt the peaceful presence of God in the chaos of the emergency.

It was a few days later when I was strong enough to get up

and enjoy our new little boy that I would notice more dramatic changes in Bill's behavior. He couldn't seem to calm himself. Something had happened in Bill during that time of stress. It made sense to me that not having control in any of the birth was hard for him, bringing back the trauma of the boulder and the fear of losing me. It seemed to increase Bill's agitation. His mania and paranoia were getting worse. I am not exactly sure what had happened. We agreed that he would make an appointment to see a doctor again soon.

Bill would never say anything about the birth except that too many people were there, and he didn't have anything to do. The midwife would never tell me all that happened, but she felt the need to tell me, "Linda, you are the strong one. Trust in yourself and follow your intuition."

That was the first time I ever heard myself described as strong. She had gotten to know us very well over recent months. Maybe she was right. Maybe I was stronger than I thought. The midwife also had set us both down and strongly warned us not to have any more children. My life was at risk with another pregnancy. Bill especially took that very seriously, as he said, "I won't risk losing her."

Benjamin was delightful! He was a fun little boy, who, from the earliest, was very different from Will. Will had chocolate brown eyes and sandy brown hair. Benjamin had white-blonde hair and bright blue eyes and the longest dark lashes. Will was methodical, where Benjamin was carefree, and he even displayed what we called baby humor from the beginning. Benjamin was a natural comic. God always gives one just what one needs. Benjamin always made me smile with his fearless activity and boundless energy. Julie was a natural nurturer to him, and he adored her.

XIV

God's Pillar

"Consider it pure joy, my brothers and sisters, whenever you face trials of many kinds."

James 1: 2 (NIV)

Will had been gone four years. Bill had become more and more short-tempered and angry. He had always had a quick fuse, but now it seemed like his explosions were more frequent without a pattern and much more violent. He was angry and bitter. He had become more critical, judgmental, and he seemed to be competing with me somehow. He would become irritated over little annoyances and then explode. I knew his father had physically abused his mother over the years, but Bill had always said, "I am not my father." I would retreat and implode in the *safe* dark room in my mind. After all, I excused him; it wasn't every day; that's what *real* abusers did, right? I understood the helplessness and pain he felt, and I had no power to erase our past from our lives. We still felt broken inside. Sometimes we would go a few months at a time without any *violent episodes*. I just never could determine what the triggers were because they seemed random. Bill never hurt the children, but his outbursts of rage were terrifying, and they were sometimes in fear of him.

Back in the early 1990s, PTSD (Post Trauma Stress Disorder) was not widely talked about unless it was in context of the military. But as I have looked back, it is easy to see that Bill had all the signs and symptoms. Because of our personal holistic belief system, we did not smoke, drink, or take medication unless necessary. I wish I could say that his episodes only took place because he drank or got high, but Bill Stapleton didn't do anything like that. He had gotten drunk one time at a party when we were first married and had suffered through bed spins that night and vowed to never drink again. He kept that promise to himself and to God as far as I know. He was never interested in smoking anything but a pipe. I remember a time he had tried *chew* from one of the heavy equipment operators that helped develop our land, and in just a few minutes, he dizzily dropped to his knees and began heaving. Even with cold medicine, he always had a hyper-reaction. I also know Bill had an extreme anxiety disorder. At least that was one doctor's diagnosis. Early on the violence had been abusive with verbal outbursts and knocking over furniture, but it wasn't long before I became the target. I found myself living a nightmare and walking on eggshells.

We had a deep commitment to God and each other. However, we were living a double life. To the outside world, we were vocal Christians, who represented God and told others how wonderful He was, but our daily lives revealed through the everyday tension and walking on eggshells that we had not experienced the true transformational power of **letting go** and **letting God** handle our pain. We had never fully turned our lives over to God, making Him Lord. Or, if we did let it go, it would only last until the next stressor, and we'd pick it up again. It was a sobering truth that as hard as we tried, we could not heal ourselves. We were the hypocrites: people who said one thing and lived another. Clearly, we needed help, and life was spinning out of control. I hated living this lie.

Bill was a health food store junkie, so he resisted my pleas to take his anti-anxiety medicine instead of herbal formulas. He had taken some meds over the years, and they seemed to help keep him more even, but he complained the whole time about a myriad of other side effects.

I left Bill a couple of times for extended stays in Jersey, but each time was sent back by pastors who strongly counseled me to be a more understanding, obedient, and submissive wife. The church, in general, clearly had a lot to learn about domestic violence.

For many survivors of trauma, they tend to live life through the lens of what they experienced, and they define themselves through that lens. The divorce rate is very high for parents who lose a young child. When two people are wounded at the same time, it is almost impossible to help each other because of their own individual pain. I knew that Bill was hurting, but I had withdrawn to protect myself. We knew we were not the same. I knew I was forgiven by God, but the weight of the shame was more than I could bear. Bill was still so angry deep inside. I remember hearing him rail at God one night out in the woods. He screamed and blamed God yelling, "You always take away everything I love!"

In a lot of ways, we were both wallowing in our own mud puddles of self-pity. It would take more time for God to reveal His truth to Bill and me. In so many ways, Bill's and my perception of what a Christian should look like and act like was as different and distorted as fun house mirrors. We only knew what we had experienced. We failed miserably and were full of inconsistencies as we desired to reflect who He was in our lives. Bill would sometimes talk about how he desired a spiritual mentor or some man from the church who could show him how to live a Christian life. We had not met any. It seemed unattainable, but God would be faithful and patient as we pursued a greater understanding of Him in our separate ways.

Over the next few years, I was getting more and more speaking engagements at churches and women's meetings. I never sought them, but I was careful to not turn them down because I believed that God's Spirit was leading each invitation. Every time I would return from a speaking engagement, I would feel a little stronger. They were good for me. I had the freedom to talk and share feelings and thoughts with godly women. I found understanding and support that I didn't have within my marriage. I felt myself healing and getting emotionally stronger. Even as I write, I marvel at how God was so faithful to give me just what I needed to heal.

Tragedy or trauma tends to shape how you live your life-long journey to survive the disease, heartache, or loss. Through my journey, I have been able to take a good hard look at my life through His eyes. From God's perspective, I have realized that my experiences don't define who I am to Him. My challenges have REVEALED who I was all along! I have been a child of God who did not know how to live as a true child of God with victory over adversity, freedom from guilt and shame, joy instead of sadness, and peace instead of depression. Over the years, I have come to realize that there are many others who haven't discovered that either.

I distinctly remember one day as I sat in on one of Julie's ballet classes. The teacher was gracefully demonstrating pirouettes, twirling around in circles from one end of the room to the other. All the young girls watched with bright hope in their eyes because they knew it was time for them to learn to do a proper pirouette. The teacher started to replay the music, and all the girls started to twirl around, and before they knew what had happened, they were dizzily bumping into each other. The teacher stopped the music and gathered them all seated in front of her. Sweetly laughing, she told them that bumping into each other would always happen because they did not know the *ballerina secret* yet. As they all scrunched forward, it was clear they all wanted to know the *ballerina secret.* She then took each one individually and had them pick a spot in the dance studio and ensure they were always looking at that spot when they turned. Then, they would never have to worry about getting dizzy or bumping into one another again. Their eyes would be focused as their head would turn back quickly to their spot.

Earlier that day I had been reading about the potter's wheel in Jeremiah, and as I read it, I had pictured myself as the shapeless lump of clay the Master potter was spinning on His wheel – a hunk of clay that had been smashed down because it wasn't quite what the Potter wanted, and now it was being spun around and reshaped, and I was feeling confused -- dizzy. But as I heard the ballet teacher explain the importance of focus, God, in His wisdom, flooded my soul, and in that moment, I realized I did not have to keep figuring everything out about God. I needed to trust His Words and focus on Him. I needed to focus on what He was saying to me and fix my eyes on Him through His Word, the Bible.

I knew intellectually that when I brought Jesus into my life, the old was gone and the new had come, but I was still daily feeding the old nature with the same old mindset of criticism, the same harsh condemnation, the shame, and judgments that I had heard during my lifetime. I did not speak His Words to myself. I would constantly compare myself to others and come up less than, putting myself down. But now, I was determined to think differently.

The Bible calls it renewing your mind because now you have the mind of Christ. I would begin an intentional effort to focus attention to how I was thinking and making sure it lined up with what God said about me. I began by talking to myself kinder and in His truth. Instead of playing old memories of harsh voices of judgment when I would make a mistake or Bill's frequent criticism and put downs, I would stop the negative memory and throw it away. Much like you would hit the button for the trash can to delete an email on your computer. I intentionally started a new vocabulary in my mind that would grace me instead of judging myself. I would remind myself that I was "fearfully and wonderfully made" and that God had a plan for me; He chose me, and I mattered to Him. He was making a way for me to come out of my darkness. By focusing on God's truth, I was using the power of God's voice to quiet and affirm my soul. Bill's critical spirit and name calling would hurt me, but I was beginning to take back the power that I had given to him to hurt me. I knew Bill loved me but was also afraid of losing me. I was moving toward God. I was leaning on Him more and making His truth my heart. I was rising above the pain. I couldn't help Bill. He had to find his way with God, too. Bill's blame was the elephant in the room, and it was choking the life out of him and our marriage.

I was gradually coming back to life in little ways. I focused on being grateful for everything we still had left. Our home was the chosen location for frequent home school outings and play dates for the kids. I became active in 4-H, hosting and teaching a group of teenage girls to learn to sew once a week after school. Doing that led to emceeing fashion shows and all the fun and planning that surrounded those events. I also had joined Extension Homemakers where I was asked to bring the devotional when we met once a month. I really enjoyed the camaraderie of the older women, and I would learn a lot from them as they shared their recipes, made crafts, organized their homes, and offered their friendship.

Bill still had his music, loved teaching his students, and got close to many of the families. I think that often it was his therapy. Sometimes he would actually come home happy. But, then other times, he would come back home, and the least little thing would set him off. It gradually got to a point where I never knew who was going to come home in the evening, Jekyll or Hyde? He became more abusive, critical, and harsh. I knew he was frustrated, angry, and hurting. By that time, I had shut down to him to protect myself and found myself distant from him. I am sure we both felt abandoned by each other. We just didn't know how to move forward together anymore.

Bill did not want to go to counseling, fearing being medicated. I just wanted us to get along better, so I surprised Bill by enrolling us in a marriage conference, thinking we might be able to find each other again. We didn't make it past the first meeting. Bill angrily stormed out of the small group time as I helplessly followed after him, humiliated by the public outburst. He was agitated and stressed most of the time. He would often split wood for hours after he got home, saying that it helped him sleep.

The most enjoyable times were when we went on outings as a

family. The children were growing up. Benjamin was almost four, and Julie was nine. Even though our relationship wasn't healthy, both of us loved being with our children. They became our *demilitarized zone*. Western North Carolina has so many beautiful places for families to visit, hike, and enjoy. The Nature Center in Asheville became a regular destination, as well as many other family friendly sites near us. We loved going out as a family and tried to do that at least one or two weekends a month. Great weekends redeemed our dysfunction. When Bill played with the kids, these were glimpses of the man I loved a long time ago.

XV

God's Purification

". . . (for the fruit of the light consists in all goodness, righ-
teousness, and truth) and find out what pleases the Lord. Have
nothing to do with the fruitless deeds of darkness, but rather
expose them. It is shameful even to mention what the disobe-
dient do in secret. But everything exposed by the light be-
comes visible—and everything that is illuminated becomes a
light. This is why it is said: 'Wake up, sleeper, rise from the
dead, and Christ will shine on you.' Be very careful, then, how
you live—not as unwise but as
wise . . . ."

Ephesians 5: 9-16 (NIV)

"I will bless you going in and I will bless you going out"

Psalm 108 (NIV)

Spending time with the Spirit of God fills one's soul with an overflow of HIS love, joy, peace, gentleness, patience, kindness, goodness, faithfulness, and self-control. These are the attributes that are listed as the fruit of the Spirit in Galatians 5:22 as a description of a mature believer in Jesus Christ. The process to become a person who exhibits the fruit of God's Spirit is one that can only be planted by God through Holy Spirit. In a similar process, it would be like seeing a tree in the winter; you may have trouble identifying it until one sees an apple or pear hanging from a branch. We are like this as we grow in God's transformational and maturing process. It is an amazing truth of nature that even though we can reproduce things through technology, we still can't make fruit. We can make just about anything fruit flavored, but it is an imitation and still not the same. No matter what we do to imitate or pretend, we still need God to produce the real fruit flavor. It is the same for the spiritual process within us. Only God can make us our true, unique, one-of-a-kind flavor.

As a family, we had been out all day with the last stop being grocery shopping. The car was loaded with groceries, and the two children had fallen asleep in the back seat. As Bill pulled up to the house and parked the car, I quickly grabbed a couple of grocery bags and rummaged in my purse to find my keys. I got to the front door, still fumbling with the groceries and my keys, and looked back over my shoulder for Bill. There he was, standing next to the car, just watching me with his keys dangling from his hand.

When I looked at him quizzically, he said, "You always do that."

"Do what?" I asked.

"You always rush ahead. I wanted to get the door and unload all the groceries, so you could help the kids. You don't ever give me a chance to help you," Bill complained.

Wow, he was so right. I hated to admit it, but he was spot on! The worst part was that I do the same thing with God! I didn't mean to hurt my husband any more than I mean to hurt God. I was sincerely trying to get it all done, but in doing so, little by little, I programmed him out of my life! I didn't act like

I was part of a team, let alone a marriage. This was a powerful teaching moment for me and an honest time of repentance with God, with myself, and with Bill. No matter what you endure in life, it takes two people to make a marriage work. God was revealing to me how I had gradually shut Bill out of my life. I had pulled in to protect myself because of his unpredictable, manic moments. I had thrown up a wall, and by this time, he was like an unpredictable guard dog I didn't trust. I knew he loved me and was loyal, but he had bitten me too many times. I never felt safe, especially when we were home alone.

Bill and I had become good friends with a local pastor and his wife, Phillip and Lynne. They were preparing to start a church plant and really wanted us to partner with them in their ministry. I knew we weren't in any shape to take on that responsibility, but I was grateful for the friendship the guys shared. I prayed that maybe Bill would open up to Phillip about his anger issues and episodes. Instead, God put another plan into action one day when Phillip and Lynne stopped by our home unexpectedly. As we were all talking, Bill flew into a rage at something I said and started to choke me in front of them. I was mortified. Bill had never *lost it* in front of anyone but the kids! After Phillip had intervened and subdued Bill, he turned to me and told me to get packed immediately: They were not going to leave the children and me alone with Bill.

Phillip emphatically stated that, and he and Lynne would protect me until Bill got some help. Even though I was humiliated, I was very relieved someone else was there to witness the violence and hold Bill accountable for his behavior. I knew Bill was damaged and hurting and not mentally stable. I loved him and shared the depth of pain and betrayal that comes through the loss of a child. I felt hope for the first time in years, so I reasoned with them. Maybe now that Bill's rage had been exposed, perhaps he would stop. They eventually, but reluctantly, allowed me to stay. Before leaving, they took me aside and clearly outlined a plan for me to execute if it ever happened again. We saw each other regularly, and Bill and I were incident-free for a couple of months.

After I had returned home from a speaking engagement, we had another night of violence. Before accepting the engagement, I had reached the point of asking God to not let any more invitations arrive because it only made things worse for Bill. It wasn't that he was resentful that he hadn't been invited to the women's events, but he had not been asked to speak at all. Bill was competitive in most things, and somehow this area of ministry was really getting to him. I think he saw that getting out and speaking was healing me, and down deep, he feared my walking away.

This episode was the worst and most violent. It even carried over into the next day. Bill woke up still agitated and angry. I hadn't even had a chance to call Phillip and Lynne. Now both of my eyes were black and blue, my nose was a bloody mess, and bruises covered much of my body. Eventually, he stormed out.

When I pulled myself together, I went to find the children to ensure they were okay. They usually hid when Bill was raging. I heard them in Benjamin's bedroom, so I just leaned against the door jam in the hall for a moment, peeking through the slightly cracked door. They were both sitting in the middle of Ben's blue race car bed. Julie was holding and rocking Benjamin under a blanket they had pulled over their heads. Julie was gently saying, "Just stay here. He'll be gone soon, and then we'll be okay."

My heart broke; I had stayed all this time for them. I felt like the roof had been pulled back to let the light come in. It hit me fully for the first time, my staying was damaging them! It didn't matter that he didn't hit them! They were being damaged by my staying! This was a defining and profound moment for me. It was in that moment of revelation that there was no turning back. I felt like God was giving me supernatural strength and a clear mind. I called to Lynne and got myself cleaned up the best I could.

We all sprang into action, following the plan we had made a few months earlier. The trunk of my car already contained the essentials. I had opened my own bank account in town and had been making weekly deposits. As calmly as I could, I told nine-year-old Julie to pack her a suitcase. She was so worried about Pepsi, our retriever, and Ribbon, her cat. It broke my heart to tell her we couldn't take them right now, but her dad would need to take care of them. I told her to sit down and write her dad a letter with instructions for their care. She promptly got some notebook paper and did that very thing. She was packed up in no time, and she even helped me get our things into the car. I knew I had some fractured ribs. I made sure she understood it may be some length of time before we could come back, so she even helped Benjamin load up his *important things,* too. My whole body ached, especially my ribs and arms, but this time no bones had actually been broken.

Within a couple of hours, we were ready to leave. I will never forget that moment. As I slowed the car at the bend of the driveway to take one last look at our mountainside home, Julie looked at me and said, "You know, Mom, you really should have done this years ago." I looked at my *wise beyond her years* little girl and said nothing. How could I ever explain to her that I stayed because I thought that was what good wives did to keep their families together? Up until this moment, I had no idea how much I had damaged her! I prayed it wasn't irreparable. I did realize we all needed help. I was overwhelmed with sadness, fear, and uncertainty for our future, but I was filled with supernatural strength and a new resolve to expose the darkness in our home. I was determined not to return until full healing could be experienced.

I was heading to the pastor's house. They were waiting for us, and by the time I got there, they had cleared out their underground garage in anticipation this would happen. They knew! I pulled the car in. The garage door descended behind us until my car was completely hidden. We were all anxious Bill would come to take me back. We were correct in our anxiety.

Later that evening he had circled the house, as well as the neighborhood, and had called Phillip. Phillip did talk with Bill, but Phillip was buying time because I was going *underground*. After Polaroid pictures were taken of my injuries for evidence in court, I called my parents. They had retired to the beach a few years earlier. Even though they were on a fixed income, they welcomed us, and they prepared to let the children and me invade their small retirement home.

Meanwhile, still in the mountains of North Carolina, the kids and I were being cared for by our dear rescuers. Phillip and Lynne helped me develop a plan for the next couple of weeks. We all slept soundly that night from sheer exhaustion. God comforted me over and over in my mind with one scripture, *"I will guard your going out and your coming in from this time forth and forever"* (Psalm 121: 8, KJV). I felt the incredible "peace that passes all understanding" as I prepared to drive the seven-hour road trip with my small, trusting children. In the morning, we said a grateful goodbye to our dear *angels in earth suits* and to North Carolina. Then we headed for the beach.

I knew Bill would assume I was headed to New Jersey. My brother-in-law had died suddenly a few months earlier in a tragic car accident, and I had been talking with my sister, Kris, regularly. It seemed logical that I would head there to be with her and my three nephews. Yet, God's Spirit was leading me, and I knew for certain I was not supposed to go north. Instead, I planned to go and live with my parents in South Carolina. Along with my sister, I also enlisted the help of my uncle in Jersey. I knew for certain Bill would call him. Uncle Frank was the key factor because Bill loved and trusted him. My uncle just wanted us to heal. The plan was simple: create the illusion I was in New Jersey. This would give me space and time to heal and think. The fourteen-hour drive was too far to drive quickly, and Bill had too many business obligations to just take off to come after me. For more than a month, it all worked splendidly!

Bill and I had friends whom I knew would never understand the depths of our dysfunction and hidden pain. They had only seen fragments. I was exhausted from trying to cover up the dark side with excuses and rationalizations. I was done now, depleted emotionally and physically. I had endured it to protect my children and family, but I had lost myself in the process. Standing on the scripture of Ephesians 5, I knew I had to *". . . expose what is done in secret . . . to live as children of the light."* I could not pretend any longer. I would not live in the darkness of our secret any longer. Bill was mentally unstable, and he needed help. I could not heal him. I could not be his strength. He needed to do this himself.

Good friends watched over him to ensure he did not hurt himself during that time, and he was directed toward sound counsel. The next time I would see him was in court, more than four weeks later.

After leaving my children with their grandparents, I drove to the women's shelter back in North Carolina, which had offered me a *pro bono* lawyer. I had to find a way to get full custody of the children. However, the interview with the attorney was not very encouraging. She explained that in the State of North Carolina, I would have to share the children 50/50 with Bill as he had not abused the children. Apparently, beating your spouse in view of your children is not abuse. They loved their dad, but they were afraid of him.

I had completed most of the paperwork by phone and now found myself in a North Carolina Family Court at a hearing to determine custody. I must admit, I really didn't care for my attorney. Her obvious distain was evidenced by her lack of empathy and respect for me. Her condescending manner let me know that in her estimation, I was the fool for staying with him. She barely tolerated my questions. In fact, in retrospect, I don't even know why she took my case. I did know I was asking God for a miracle, a BIG miracle. I just needed to have full custody of my children, and the only One who could deliver that was God. After all, the impossible is what He does best. Waiting alone in a room adjacent to the court, it finally came time for my case to be heard.

Bill arrived with no attorney. He looked horrible, thinner, and unshaven. He and my attorney were summoned to the bench. They stood in front and conversed with the Judge, but I could not hear a thing. As soon as they returned to their seats, the Judge spoke.

He first addressed Bill. "Mr. Stapleton, it is my understanding you are waiving your rights for custody of your children?"

"Yes sir," Bill replied.

Then the Judge replied sternly, "I don't want to see you back here in a couple of weeks changing your mind. Do you understand?"

"Yes sir," `Bill replied. "I need to get help, and she's a far better parent than I am."

"So, it is. Mrs. Stapleton has full custody!" the Judge ordered, as the gavel struck the bench. I was stunned! But actually, I believe my attorney seemed more stunned.

Bill immediately left the courtroom, so we never spoke a word to each other. I followed my attorney to a back room to sign some additional papers. I knew the fullness and favor of God's love. He had given me a miracle and was making a way for us to heal. I could trust in Him and not be afraid.

I saw Bill the next afternoon when I returned to the house to get a few more things. I was accompanied by a police escort and a restraining order. The first item on the list was Pepsi, our family dog. The kids missed her so much. They affectionately called her *Pepsi-Nana*, like the dog in *Peter Pan*. She was always with them. As soon as she saw me, she tried to get into the car, searching for *her* kids. I couldn't bring Ribbon because Granma was allergic, but Ribbon seemed to understand and hid the whole time.

This time it was hard. The police kept Bill from coming near me, so he just stood there with tears rolling down his face. For the first time in a very long time, I didn't cry. Maybe Bill would get better, maybe not, but I was going to do all I could to heal and ensure our children were healthy. Emotionally exhausted, I drove back to the beach. I was relieved and thanking God with my whole heart for His miraculous intervention. For now, I had my babies, and I was "living by faith and not by sight."

I felt like everything in my life that mattered to me was broken: my family, my marriage, my heart, my soul, and even my faith. I knew I needed healing. One morning I asked my mother whether she knew of a church that had a Bible study. She said her little church did not have one, but she remembered that a lady in the carpet store where they had just bought carpeting had a Bible on her desk. Mom then gave me the number to the carpet store. I called the woman there and told her I needed to find a Bible study group.

She was silent for a minute and then she said, "I will call you back in two days." I thanked her and trusted that I would hear back from her. I would find out several years later, when I met the woman, and when I had asked her my question, she heard the Spirit say, "Not your Bible Study." She said to me later that she was willing to take me to hers, but it was a distance away, and she heard God clearly say that He wanted her to find me another.

God is so real, and yes, people really do hear from Him. True to her word to me, she gave me a call back in two days with two phone numbers. One was a church number, and the other was a sweet lady named Laura. I called Laura. We talked over an hour and a half! She had been through some similar circumstances and was anxious to help me, but her Bible study was ending that week. I was disappointed until she said she was going to another Bible study starting up for the summer. It wasn't through her church, but through a friend's. I never did call the church number because in two weeks, I would meet my new friend face-to-face and become part of a network of amazing Christian women. I would end up being immersed in the fellowship and love of dear women who loved God. They went to a thriving Community Church that met in a high school auditorium. I was introduced to a counselor named Joyce. She and her husband John, who also served as the church administrator, represented a Para Church Ministry called Victorious Christian Living International, based in Phoenix Arizona, and that was the name of the Bible Study in which I was already enrolled.

I started regular counseling with Joyce. She became my mentor and my friend. Through her gentle patience and Godly teaching, I began to realize that God had not wasted any of the heartache or the tears. He was beginning to restore what I thought had been lost and make me whole through all my mess. I also knew I was in the middle of a divine intervention. I would find myself knowing that even though Bill and I had been able to forgive murderers, we had been unable to forgive ourselves and each other. I would become part of a restorative process to be able to release myself and Bill from the shame and guilt we felt. We had locked ourselves in a prison of unforgiveness all these years because of our shameful past.

Through counseling, God was helping me learn more about who He was and who I wasn't. God our Creator doesn't think like us, or act like us. He has a much BIGGER perspective of our world and His ultimate purpose for each of us. The very reason He sent a Savior was because He knew we all needed a way back to the Father. Even when I didn't feel Him, I knew He hadn't left me. Not only because I believed God's Word was truth, but also because I remember reading in the Psalms that

King David, many times, had called God "the God who hides from me," and I would childishly comfort myself by believing that this was like the childhood game of hide and seek, where He would be hiding, but watching me from right around the corner.

Suffering is a mystery to me, much like God Himself at times, and through Job's story, I came to respect the mystery. His ways are not our ways. His thoughts are not our thoughts as it states in Isaiah 55:8. I still can't explain why children die or why there is cancer, cruelty, injustice, or crime. I do know that only the One who created me could use my circumstances to not only bring me closer to Him, but to restore me to wholeness. I know that I found myself partnering with Job in this mystery of God, a mystery that brought me into the very presence of childlike wonder, love, peace, and praise when one lets go of the *why* and lets God be God. I stepped aside and let God be BIGGER. It was His rightful place because He created me and knew me best.

I know that I asked the question "Why," far too many times with no satisfaction until it registered with me one day that the only answer to the "Why" was a simple, "Because I AM God, and you are not." The same way I, *as Mommy*, would sometimes answer my children's relentless questions of *why?* Because I am the Mom! I love you; that is why! My children had to learn to trust me just like I had to trust in a BIGGER GOD, a God who loved me and had more of a plan for my life than I could ever fathom. I was just a screaming, crying, helpless, little child, and HE wanted to be my daddy. I would begin to see HIM very differently. My questions now became more like the questions asked by the early church at Pentecost: "What does this mean?" and "What shall we do?"

God wanted a relationship with me that went beyond trying

too hard to please or do good things for others. He wanted me to know that no matter how I would fall short of HIM, I was still HIS BELOVED, I was HOLY, I was BLESSED, I was ADOPTED into HIS family, I was CHOSEN, I was BLAMELESS, and I was FORGIVEN.

No one could shame me again by pointing out my faults in judgment because I was His child. I was bought with a great price, the blood of Jesus. His voice had become the loudest voice in my head. His was the voice of truth. Yes, He knows all the ways I fall short of His perfect law, and yet, He still wants an intimate relationship with me! He wants me! I have been forgiven so much! It would be this very piece of the puzzle in my quest that gave reason to why God sent me hurling back from Heaven to understand and to tell others. I had been on a quest all these years to find out and accept who I was in Him! I couldn't find my true *self* because I was always getting in God's way by trying to do the right thing instead of being the right person. I thought the best I did, the better it would make me feel, and He would love me more, as if sending His only Son wasn't enough.

GOD thinks BIGGER than the greatest mind or computer on the planet. He knows each one of us better than we know ourselves, even down to the number of hairs on our heads. He doesn't think like us; He thinks far beyond us! He doesn't work out problems logically like we do; instead, He uses ways we avoid like loss, tragedy, betrayal, disappointment, and pain to unravel us, causing us to question Who He is and to find Him.

After being separated a few months, Bill would begin to call once a week to talk to me and the children. At first, it was more like a report of his doctor and counseling appointments, always ending with begging me to come back home. He sent money regularly; he said he would do whatever it took to get his family back.

I had no intentions of returning to the marriage or the mountains, but I did want him to get well. My children needed a healthy father. Every night, as we said bedtime prayers, I would ask Julie to pray for her dad, realizing I was still too hurt and angry over all the damage we were living in. For now, I just wanted to stay separated forever. The children were doing very well. For the first time in years, there was no stress and no tension. They were happy at Granma's and Granpa's. Benjamin had a little friend in the neighborhood, too. Both Julie and Benjamin swam like guppies in the neighbors' pool every day. I continually prayed that they would be protected from the evil one, and that "no root of bitterness would spring up in them" (based on Hebrews 12:15). God seemed to be keeping them healthy and happy.

They were surrounded with lots of love within the church, and Julie was even getting counsel from another dear woman named Linda from the church, too. Many times, they would meet at the mall or at the park, and Julie was thriving. Both children missed their dad very much, and I knew especially at bedtime that through Julie's sweet, heartfelt prayers, somehow God would heal us. Bill would now call and talk to them often saying he would come to see them soon when he got well. Months later I would look on the note I had scribed with the two phone numbers, and as you might have guessed, the other number was the church where we already were. God was guiding each step of the way.

XVI

God'S Purpose

"I will give you a new heart and put a new spirit in you; I will remove from you your heart of stone and give you a heart of flesh."

Ezekiel 36:26 (NIV)

The next six months flew by quickly. The children and I were making new friends; I was going to counseling and pursuing my relationship with God in a discipleship class. Bill and I did not have physical contact since that day in court. It was only through friends and his phone calls that I knew that he had been consistent in getting help. He had one counselor in Asheville and then another one in Rutherfordton. When he called the children, I would sometimes talk to him briefly and marvel at the brokenness and tender repentance genuinely expressed, but it did not draw me back in. I was encouraged because I wanted a healthy father for our children, but I was resolute in my decision not to go back to him or the remote mountain side. Over these months, I had also learned more about domestic violence. Two key elements for the behavior were first, having it modeled within the family of origin and second, isolating the family from their support network. Since Bill had grown up with an abusive father, and we were so far away from family, I was determined to never risk putting myself in that situation ever again.

It would also take much more than merely expressing his

sorrow. He would need to show and prove it through his actions. At this point, he started to travel from the mountains to the beach once a month to see the children. They would stay with him at his hotel and have fun with him in the hotel pool or at the beach, but I never joined them. Julie and Benjamin eagerly looked forward to his fun visits. Over the next few months, he started coming every other weekend, and occasionally, we would all play putt putt together or go out to dinner and a movie. Bill and I were cordial again, and we were talking more. We were rebuilding an understanding of ourselves, as well as our faith, but we were not working on reconciling our marriage.

We went back to basic core beliefs about our human nature. It all goes back to the beginning of humanity in the Garden of Eden, when God came down and gave Adam three opportunities to admit and take responsibility for his sin. We could identify with the darkness of our humanness when first, there was denial, second, a cover-up, and third, the blame game. When all God really wanted was for Adam to take responsibility for his sinful actions. We would have to learn about God's unconditional love first instead of being afraid of Him.

It only makes sense that to have true intimacy with your Creator there must be no secrets between you and God. It's not that He doesn't already know the good, the bad, and the ugly. After all, He created you. He does know you better than you know yourself. Then, when you have come before Him honest, broken, and undone, not excusing or justifying behavior, but agreeing with Him by admitting to Him your character flaws and transgressions, then the relationship sweetens, and the grace begins to flow.

The ground is leveled at the foot of the cross. There is

none without sin. We all stand in need of Him. Both Bill and I had to own our part in our mess. It is only after we stop shifting the blame to others, God, or ourselves for our shortcomings and stop trying to rationalize and justify our wrongs that we can finally begin to experience the powerful reality of a supernatural ability to demonstrate a supernatural love. God is still the only one who can make genuine fruit. Humanity can only manufacture "fruit flavor." Love generated by the Holy Spirit is the true love that you cannot fake, a genuine love, an authentic abiding joy, undeniable peace, goodness, kindness, patience, gentleness, meekness, and self-control. Love is more powerful than evil.

Love never gives up.
Love cares more for others than for self.
Love doesn't want what it doesn't have.
Love doesn't strut,
Doesn't have a swelled head,
Doesn't force itself on others,
Isn't always 'me first,'
Doesn't fly off the handle,
Doesn't keep score of the sins of others,
Doesn't revel when others grovel,
Takes pleasure in the flowering of truth,
Puts up with anything,
Trusts God always,
Always looks for the best,
Never looks back,
But keeps going to the end. Love never dies.
1 Corinthians 13:4-8, (MSG)

Operating in His power, one is then empowered to forgive others as HE forgave mankind. We had forgiven murderers; we knew we could forgive each other, but it would take more of a process this time. God is Supernatural. HE is in the business of miracles and healings. We are made in HIS image, yet we remain in the natural and unchanged until we become inhabited by the HIS power, THE HOLY SPIRIT, the third person in the Godhead. One can modify behavior through education and therapy, but the only way to experience heart change is to believe and trust in the SON of God. One must take Jesus at His word when HE says, *"I am the way, the truth and the life; no one can come to the Father except by ME"* John 14:6 (NIV).

If we had the ability to reach God without Jesus, we would all be perfect; Jesus, the perfect sacrifice, would willingly take our place and shed His blood for our sins. We would still be trying to keep all the rules and pay for our sins with the life and blood of a dead animal. Instead, Jesus totally graced and redeemed us by laying down HIS perfect life so that we could have a new and doable life. Through Christ we are given a new life that is evidenced by freedom to be who He created me to be, evidenced by new, healthy fruit, fruit that is sweet and amazingly good even when squeezed.

Would I ever be able to fully trust Bill? Probably not. But I would be able to see the evidence of God's Spirit in his life if he was genuinely changing. The Bible says it this way:

> *But when anyone turns to the Lord, the veil is taken away. Now the Lord is the Spirit, and where the Spirit of the Lord is, there is freedom.*

And we who with unveiled faces all reflect the Lord's glory, are being transformed into His likeness with ever-increasing glory, which comes from the Lord, who is the Spirit.

2 Corinthians 3:16-18, (NIV)

Jesus' death kills one's old self, and we get a new self supernaturally through the Spirit. The fruit of the Spirit are evidenced and present a sweet vibe when a person is spiritually intimate with his/her Creator.

Bill was healing from the inside out, and so was I. I was experiencing the grace of God in a spectacular and life-changing way through a class called VCL or Victorious Christian Living.

I expressed to Bill that I wished he could take the same twelve-week Victorious Christian Living Class I was getting ready to take again. By this time, I knew I wanted to learn everything the classes offered. The classes were clearing up so much of the confusion and contradictions I had experienced through traditional Christianity. I was astonished when he began to travel seven hours each way every weekend to be with us and take the class. I recognized that Bill was doing all he could to prove he would make every effort to become a husband, father, and man who was God-honoring and healthy.

When Bill played with the kids, these were glimpses of the man I loved a long time ago. God was stirring up embers of warmth inside my cold, icy heart with the man I fell in love with a lifetime ago. I wasn't tempted one bit to go back to the mountains though; I know Bill was heart sick as I told him with resolve that I would not go back there to live. I knew that I would never feel safe there, and we would lose the accountability network we had established at the beach. I also sensed this was spiritual test. I earnestly believed God was calling me to train with Victorious Christian Living International (VCLI), which would mean going to Phoenix, Arizona, or Opelika, Alabama. At that time, I also thought that would never happen with Bill by my side.

I did trust that God would make our future clear by the time we needed to hear from Him. As we talked about what to do next, Bill was more open and willing for God to lead than I ever would have imagined. By the end of the class, he announced that he had closed up his shop and his teaching in North Carolina. This radical news melted my heart. I knew Bill was giving up everything he dreamed and had poured his life into. Bill was trusting God to make the way.

I finally trusted I could go back into my marriage because it would be a different marriage with two different and improved people in it. We were working hard at functioning as a team. We wanted a marriage in which both of us were transforming and healing in Him. We had been learning better coping and communication skills, and I was clearly hearing God tell me to trust Him with Bill. I was asking God to help me love Bill through His Spirit and asking God to help me see and love Bill through His eyes. I could trust the Spirit I saw within Bill, and I again remembered the trip to Heaven, entreating me to follow Bill.

Bill was emotionally and spiritually doing much better, but physically, all the stress and travel were wearing on him. A hard lump had suddenly appeared on his neck during the holidays. We asked for prayer and called for the Elders to pray with him, and when he went to the doctor, it was treated with penicillin. It disappeared over the next two weeks. We really thought that Bill at forty-five was just run-down from the past year.

We knew God was leading and guiding our family as we decided to take this huge leap of faith. As we told the children, "We are all going on a *Spiritual Adventure*." Yes, we were fully committed to finishing this training we had started at the beach. We both wanted our family to be whole again.

When our church family found out we had decided to study further at the VCLI branch office in Alabama, they not only rejoiced with us, but the mission board decided to invest in our lives by providing us with some monthly financial support toward our schooling. We were shocked, deeply touched, and profoundly encouraged. We were surprised and humbled by the church's love and support. It had never even occurred to us to ask for their help. We still were very independent in our thinking. We had a couple of year's salary in savings, and we were certain that, whatever it took, God would supply. After all, He always had. It was a brand-new season for our family.

Not everyone was happy about us leaving to go to Opelika, Alabama. My parents were very wary, but I have always known that they believed in me and, even more importantly, in God's presence in my life. I also knew for a fact that as they went to sleep every night, they would be praying for us. I had to trust that God was leading us, and even if I couldn't fully trust Bill yet, I could fully trust God about my relationship with Bill.

We left right after the Christmas holidays, winterizing the home in the mountains and then heading to Alabama. Even as I write about this, I can hardly believe we did it. It was a very bold leap of faith, especially for timid me, but I think that sometimes when one absolutely knows that God is speaking, one can just step out and trust that the road ahead will be clear. I could relate to the Apostle Paul when he uses the word "compelled" in 2 Corinthians 12:10-13 (NIV): *"I have become a fool in boasting; you have compelled me."*

The wording in *The Message* relays how I felt: ". . . then He (God) told me (Linda), 'My grace is enough; it's all you need. My strength comes into its own in your weakness.'" Once I heard that, I was glad to let it happen. I quit focusing on the handicap (our problems) and began appreciating the gift (of healing and starting over). It was a case of Christ's strength moving in on my weakness. Now I take limitations in stride, and with good cheer, these limitations that cut me down to size -- abuse, accidents, opposition, bad breaks. I just let Christ take over! And so, the weaker I get, the stronger I become. Well, now I've done it! I've made a complete fool of myself by going on like this. But it's not all my fault.

I love the way *The Message* reads because it tells others how vulnerable I feel in relating this. In full context, it is the Apostle Paul's explanation of his troublesome "thorn in the flesh." I knew my past would be my thorn because nothing could really change it. I would never be able to have the *do-over* I longed for, and I would never hold my child again, but I had to believe that somewhere in all the rubble of our lives, if we endured, something healthy and different would emerge.

We arrived in Opelika, Alabama, to begin a new season of reconciliation for our reunited family. The training center was an old but charming turn-of-the-century Victorian style house converted to office and classroom space. I had grown up in a three-story Victorian beach house on a barrier island in New Jersey, so it felt very welcoming to me. It was located right next to the church and served as additional space for the thriving ministry. It would become *our home away from home.*

The director and staff were ready for us at the headquarters, and we began classes in the New Year. When we first arrived, we stayed with the director of the center and then moved into the pastor's basement apartment for a short time. We spent our days in classes at the Training / Discipleship Center.

The training was rich and full, and the team of trainers poured out their hearts and love on us. There was accountability, a lot like spiritual parenting, and, in a way, it was like living in a spiritual climate-controlled terrarium. Our training dealt with all areas of life, spiritual, psychological, social, physical, financial, marital, and parental. It was called SALT, which stood for Seven Areas of Life Training. We each were assigned a trainer with intense accountability. Bill and I were challenged and stretched, but we were sure that we were where we needed to be.

We enrolled the children in their schools. This was difficult for me, especially because I had been their constant companion since birth and because the past years had been so tumultuous.

Benjamin had just turned five, and I felt he seemed *too young* to start school, so I was totally unprepared for his first day when Bill and I took him to the elementary school. Stunned, I watched him take the teacher's hand and never even turn around to say *good-bye.* He just marched right off, never looking back, only excited to see what the day would hold. I, on the other hand, was the one who fell apart. Obviously, it was the right thing to do. He thrived! Benjamin managed to be student of the week and month many times that year with lots of favor from teachers and classmates. Even at five he was good, strong, independent, and confident in his own skin.

Julie, on the other hand, had a rougher adjustment. She

had always been homeschooled because of her hearing disability, and so we decided that the smaller and quieter private Christian school would be the best thing for her. She had received a full scholarship anonymously, so we fully believed it was God making the way for her, but to say it was one of the most traumatic years of her life would be an understatement. She was in a class full of boys -- just her and one other girl. She was on the back end of her parents' chaos and now was thrown into a fourth-grade class of *terrorists*. I'm sure she would relate more detail, but it is enough for the reader to know this was an unusually rough year for my little girl. I found myself questioning God many times for the pain Julie was experiencing, but in His goodness, He had also provided a respite for her away from the classroom in the form of another family.

The Thomas family offered their friendship and their fun, welcoming home, complete with kids of the same ages, a pond to swim in, animals to love on, and even an emu! Being out in the country, it became a treasured haven through the future months. Benjamin, of course, was always happy to be where Julie was. We had been meeting wonderful families through the church next door to the center, and they provided friendships for us all but especially for Julie and Benjamin.

We were embraced by our Sunday school class, and they became our social network, opening their hearts and lives to us. It was through them that we moved into a quaint little farmhouse that used to be a dairy farm. Moving gave us more privacy and a wonderful place for the kids to play. It was even walking distance to a fully stocked fishing pond where we would take the kids to just kick back and throw the lines in. It was also where Benjamin and I dug up his first *dinosaur* bone, which totally fed his dinosaur fascination.

We discovered that a new way of life was developing for us. Bill and I functioned more like a team with the help of wise counsel. We were unlearning old behaviors and applying spiritual truths. We were practicing spiritual disciplines, such as, *taking our thoughts captive* and identifying *stinking thinking* from our families of origin as we compared it to God's Word. We had been working on Bill taking on more of the disciplining of the children because previously he had left it all up to me. Bill had been afraid that in his anger, he might escalate and hurt the kids like he had hurt me in the past. God was also teaching me to trust Him with Bill and not try to overly protect the children.

We weren't without our tests though, and I will always remember a typical evening meal after a full day of school for the kids and training for us when Benjamin was really acting out. He was cranky, tired, and not eating his dinner. Bill and I were trying to apply right parenting techniques, but I could tell Bill's temper was rising, and I knew Julie was sensing it, too. Those old vibes and triggers are hard to ignore. This was a test. Bill finally couldn't take Benjamin's behavior anymore and grabbed him up out of his chair and headed to the bathroom to apply "some *understanding* to the seat of disobedience."

His quick movement caused the chair to tip backward and make a loud crash as he carried Ben off to the nearby bathroom. My nerves were frazzled, but I got up and picked up the chair and sat back down as Julie and I braced for the worst and for even more noise to come.

After a few ominous moments of silence with no breathing or speaking, Julie and I exchanged questioning looks. A minute or two later a subdued Benjamin and Bill appeared, and they sat down and finished their dinners. Julie and I just kept flashing questioning *looks* to Bill, but he seemed determined not to speak to keep from laughing. I could hardly wait to hear what had transpired! Dinner wrapped up quickly, and Bill hung back to help me clear the table. The kids ran into the living room. Bill then burst out laughing.

He composed himself to begin by saying, "I'm sorry; I was so angry. As I headed to the bathroom with Ben, I did remember to take some deep breaths. By the time I got him to stand still and get his hands out of the way, I was just about ready to wallop him with the bamboo spoon when Benjamin looks up at me and asks, 'Dad, don't you think we should pray about this first?' I stopped in the heat! It was all I could do to keep from laughing. Out of the mouths of babes! What could I do after that? I just sat down on the toilet, put him on my lap, and we prayed."

Bill and I shared the laugh in sheer relief, and it still makes me smile because we realized it really was that simple. God just wants us to come to Him first, and HE will do the rest.

XVII

God's Pardon and Plan

"Therefore, he had to be made like his brothers in every respect, so that he might become a merciful and faithful high priest in the service of God, to make propitiation for the sins of the people. For because he himself has suffered when tempted, he is able to help those who are being tempted."

Hebrews 2:17-18 (ESV)

Bill's physical health, however, was becoming an issue again. He was having such bad back pain that he would sleep sitting up in a chair at the kitchen table. I was very concerned. He was going regularly to a chiropractor with no relief. Then, on a Monday, he dropped me off at the office and went to a doctor that he had talked to at church that Sunday. He was gone most of the day, just calling to say they were going to run some tests at the hospital, and I would have to find a way to pick up the children when school was dismissed. Borrowing a car, I went to pick up the kids, and when I got back to the training center, the children were whisked away from me, and I was told that Bill needed to see me in the director's office. One look at Bill as I walked in made me freeze in my steps as he came towards me with anguish written all over his face. I had no clue what was happening.

His words were coming out between sobbing ". . .

sonogram . . . full of tumors . . . lymphoma . . . cancer . . . biopsy . . . too many tumors to count!"

I felt like I wanted to run, but instead I stood still and held him as he sobbed. I didn't even run to the room in my head. I didn't need to run anywhere but to my Lord on His throne. Instead, I tried to wrap my brain around the information. Surely, this wasn't a death sentence. *Lord, this is just another test of our faith, right? We believe You are the Healer. I know You can heal. We are going to walk this out as we hold onto You.* Surely, we were going to see a supernatural healing. Bill hadn't been sick a day in his life. He was as healthy as any forty-five-year-old man could be, given the circumstances. The doctor had already scheduled a biopsy in Birmingham for the next week.

Somehow, we got home; the children were at the Thomas's, safe and protected. After the initial shock, I started to fight the fears that were assaulting me feverishly. *We don't have any health insurance or life insurance. How will we pay for all of this? We aren't done. What about our training?* I couldn't face the fact that Bill might die. In fact, I believed he was not going to die. Surely, God wouldn't have had us go through all we had been through and then take Bill. I just wasn't there yet. Bill wasn't saying much, and I didn't know what to say or what to think. We agreed that we would have to tell the kids that Daddy was sick but not that he might die.

I called my parents and John and Joyce. I knew our church at the beach would be praying. That Sunday, at church, we called for the Elders to lay hands on and pray for Bill. I will always remember the sermon that Sunday was on my life verse that I took so many years ago at college: Isaiah 40:31. *"They that wait upon the Lord will renew their strength, they will mount up with wings like eagles, run and not be weary, walk and not faint"* (KJV). Here we go again,

Lord. I will wait on you. Help me not to be afraid.

We drove to Birmingham three days later, and Bill had the biopsy. Two days after the biopsy, the doctor called with the lab results. It was an aggressive lymphoma, and it had clearly metastasized across Bill's diaphragm. It was typed and staged as "diffuse large cell lymphoma" moving into the fourth and last stage. Bill went back to his doctor that discovered it and asked him for the *bottom line*, to clearly state the options, and the doctor basically said, "If the cancer doesn't kill you, the chemo will." But we believed that our God of miracles could do anything. We had to trust Him. We had already walked through so much.

We now found ourselves at another crossroad. Bill was strongly resisting chemotherapy and wanted to try an alternative treatment called hydrotherapy to boost his immune system. Simply stated, it means the person is immersed into a very hot tub of water, and they try to induce a fever in hopes that your immune system can be jumpstarted. We traveled to a place down in Alabama that specialized in this type of treatment. It was very expensive, but we felt like it was worth it if it worked. They were kind enough to train me to do what they were doing for Bill, so I could do it for him at home. It was so painful for him, and we did it as often as he could stand it, but it was not working. Time was not on our side. Our life savings were quickly dwindling, and Bill was in more and more pain.

We were determined to finish our training unless God directed otherwise. God had placed us amid an amazing body of believers. Over the next month, our friends in Alabama poured out their love on us through prayer, meals, play dates for the children, groceries, and even a company gas card. We went on a family camping trip with our Sunday school class to a state park, and it almost felt like we were *normal* for a brief weekend. Our lives were far from normal though. Life was becoming a nightmare that would not end, even in the light of day.

Bill called a doctor friend of ours in North Carolina and told him his situation. Our friend had a colleague who was an oncologist, practicing in Asheville and willing to take Bill on as a patient. We knew that we would have to get Bill to Asheville, North Carolina, because that was where our legal, permanent residency was. But what would we do about the children? Bill was losing weight fast and in so much pain. We didn't have time to get them to their grandparents at the beach, so we had to leave them behind with the Thomas family. Mom and Dad would drive to Alabama in a few days and collect the children. We had no idea how long we would be gone; it was urgent that we leave as soon as we could. We didn't even know where we were going to stay once, we arrived.

That night, God woke me up. I heard His voice call my name, and I quickly grabbed the note pad and a pen by our bed as I ran into the adjacent bathroom, so I wouldn't disturb Bill with a light. It was an audible voice!

Oh, my beloved daughter, you are a pearl of great price. I am deepening your faith. I am loving you. Listen to My commands. You are to love Me with all your might, soul, and mind. You are to love others as you love yourself. Do not be afraid – trust Me that your days may be well with you. Go forth quickly; follow Bill. I will bring you out of this pain. Hear Me, hear Me now, for I Am the Lord thy God.

I even kept on writing as I questioned, *Father, did I get it written down right? Please answer me.*

He replied, "Yes, my daughter."

We were very familiar with Lake Junaluska because we had done worship music for numerous conferences there. We called the conference center, but there were no rooms available because their huge annual missions conference, when missionaries gather from all over the world at Lake Junaluska, was taking place that week leaving no vacancies. Bill then called a friend near there, and they gave him a contact number of an elderly lady named Shirley, who had a home on the lake.

She talked with Bill a few minutes and said, "Sure, just come on. I will have a room all ready for you. I won't be home to greet you, but the key is under the mat at the back door. Just let yourselves in, and I will see you in the morning."

Bill was in too much pain to drive. Instead, I made him as comfortable as I could with a bed in the back seat. We left Opelika and had to go around Atlanta's beltway that sunny morning. I will never forget my death grip on the steering wheel and the terror I felt as a huge tractor trailer barreled down upon us, passing me on the right at breakneck speed. As it overtook me, it completely obliterated the sun and left us in total dark for a few moments. I kept the wheel steady and breathed again after it passed as I heard God whispering to me that this was exactly what we were going through. We were in the shadow of death but untouched, to not "fear evil for God was with us." I had to believe that Bill would not be touched by death, and I knew for certain in that moment that God was taking us back to North Carolina His way.

Little did I know that Shirley would soon become *my Jesus*

with skin on. She was a sweet and wise widow, whose husband, Tony, had died of cancer several years earlier. She was so welcoming and truly gifted in hospitality. We felt embraced and nurtured in God's love from the first moment of meeting her.

I knew Bill depended on me more than ever now. Mom and Dad had traveled to Alabama and collected the children. They were settled back in at the beach where they were warmly welcomed by their dear Pepsi-Nana, our beloved family dog, and their network of friends in the church and neighborhood. Everything was uncertain, but for now, we agreed my parents would bring them for a visit as soon as they could.

Shortly after we got to North Carolina, we had no sooner started the chemo process when Bill had to be hospitalized. I was so scared that this was the end. He was in so much pain. I stayed all night with him at Mission Memorial Hospital. I was missing the kids and feeling very alone. Bill was in writhing pain and in and out of consciousness. Bill's sensitivity and side effects to the pain medicines kept all the nurses and doctors scrambling.

After a sleepless night, curled up in a chair, I got a call from a social worker saying that we had to talk about how we were going to pay the hospital bill. I knew our savings were almost depleted by this time and would learn that the state could take our property because we weren't living on it. I had no idea of what to do. Maybe we were supposed to lose it all -- everything we had worked for.

Bill was finally sleeping, so I walked out of his hospital room for a change of scenery. Across the waiting area, I watched the elevator doors open and out walked John and Joyce from the beach. What an amazing moment of pure love! God had them show up in a space and time that could only have been

Benjamin was born in 1991, one week before Julie turned five. A couple of family pictures through 1997. We are at Grandfather Mountain and the Blue Ridge Mountains.

orchestrated from above. In sheer relief and joy, I dissolved in tears and eventually sobbed out the situation we were facing. Not feeling quite so alone, their presence refreshed me with hope. I imagined the relief I felt was much like the Cavalry arriving in the old Western movies, when certain massacre seemed eminent.

They tenderly questioned me about the circumstances I found myself in. After listening carefully, John asked me to get him a piece of paper from the nurses' station, which I promptly did. In the time they were there, they helped me get Bill's terminal diagnosis to the Social Security Office to file for his disability, and then John, who in a *former season of life* was a union negotiator, drafted a binding agreement after a few calls to a couple of friends. The document he drew up repurposed our home and the fifteen acres bordering the Pisgah National Forest to a hunting lodge, and then he rented it out. With that piece of paper, he saved our idyllic home site from being taken by the state, and he had a great place to hunt with his buddies.

By the end of that week, Bill would be released. He was still very weak, but by staying at Lake Junaluska, his spirit was renewed, and he seemed to be regaining strength. The chemo was brutal, and with each round, he was holding his own but not really improving. Over the next few months, Shirley became my close companion. Because her husband had died of cancer years before, she would be used by God to teach me about loving and giving more. We knew when we met each other that it was a God appointment. We would laugh and say that even with our age difference, we felt like we had known each other our whole lives.

One day comes to mind as Bill stumbled and fell coming into the kitchen. I was upset with him for not using a cane and overwhelmed with the feeling of helplessness as I was watching him rapidly decline. The tumors were causing paralysis of his left side, and his condition only seemed to be worsening. I was so scared that he might die and leave us, especially now that our marriage had been put back together. It seemed especially cruel. I was upset and fussing at Bill. I know Shirley heard me. At the time, she didn't say anything, but later she would take me aside and tell me in her gentle way that she wished she had let *her Tony* do for himself more. She told me it was more important that Bill keep up the effort and that I only needed to be there to help him up when he fell. Simply because he was a man, I needed to allow Bill his dignity. She was so wise. I loved Shirley. God used her to help me "let go and let God" as she mothered both of us. She helped me see that His ways were not like ours and that God was always a just God. Even in the storms of life, He was still the only one with the true perspective and all the knowledge. Shirley was my earth angel.

The kids were visiting us almost every other weekend. People from our church were taking turns bringing them up to be with us, and it helped us all to not feel so fragmented. The hallowedness of the beautiful mountain setting was wonderful, but the goodbyes to the children got harder and harder. I remember walking around the lake one day after they left and crying out to God in anger and self-pity. "You have taken all my children away from me. Will this torture never end?" It was when I returned from my walk, emotionally exhausted, that God would direct me to a table by the rocker on the front porch to a scripture already marked in my open Bible. It was Psalm 84:1-3, (NKJV)

"How lovely is Your tabernacle O Lord of hosts.
My soul longs, yes, even faints for the courts of

the Lord; My heart and my flesh cry out for the
living God. Even the sparrow has found a home,
And the swallow a nest for herself, where she may
lay her young. Even Your altars, O lord of hosts,
My King and my God."

From that day forward, I would picture my Julie and Benjamin as small sparrows that I willingly placed in a nest, a nest right next to the altar with God. He was with them. I would have to trust Him to be comforting my children and providing for their needs. I was not given possession; they were His first. I would learn to trust as I held my children loosely on an open hand. I would continue to be grateful for such selfless and loving parents who lived to serve God.

I would often send the children cards with a pack of gum, with the sticks shaped into a man with a silly, happy moon-face and a reminder that when they looked up at the moon, I was looking up, too. On Bill's good days at the Lake Conference Center, we volunteered as greeters for events and the dining room. We met the challenges of fighting a horrible disease together. There was no other way to cope through that summer except one day at a time.

Before we knew it, it was time for the kids to enroll in school at the beach, so my mother registered them in a nearby elementary school. At least they were together in the same school this time, and they came home to Pepsi-Nana every day. We wanted to be together and missed them so much.

Bill was as desperate as any forty-five-year-old man would be to hang on to his life. He had done everything possible with God to earn his family back. He had undergone and endured nine rounds of *CHOP* (his chemo regimen), survived two more near-death hospital episodes, and yet once again he was being tested to the very depths of his soul. Bill had finally finished the chemo and was feeling better but weak.

Earlier in that day, he had said, "Let's drive down to the beach. Ben has a soccer game, and I want to surprise him!"

In no time at all, I had us packed and ready. We really had been living out of suitcases anyway. The darkest hours of the night seemed to be the hardest for Bill. In the middle of the night, I woke up to the muffled sound of heavy sobbing. Bill was seated at the bottom of our bed with his head in his hands as he heaved in sobs of despair. As I scrambled down to him, I pulled the covers with me, wrapping us up in the top blanket.

"Honey, you are on the upside now. Your numbers are better, and I just know God is going to heal you," I softly encouraged. "Are you in pain? Can I get you something?"

He only shook his head to the negative as he sighed heavily and said, "You just don't get it, Lin. I am damaged, too damaged. Please go back to sleep; you need your sleep."

I gently spoke, "I know that God is Bigger than this." But I was thinking, *We are all damaged. No one is too damag*ed. I backed away and curled up in the remaining cover. "Are you sure you don't want to talk about this?" I queried sleepily

"No," Bill replied. "You will be driving in the morning. Get your rest. Go back to sleep, please."

We never spoke again of that last night in Lake Junaluska, but looking back, I can see that it was another turning point for Bill and his healing. We left early the next morning. As we came down the mountain highway heading toward the East Coast, we saw a beautiful double rainbow. It felt so promising!

We went straight to the soccer field. The drive took a lot

out of Bill, so much that he couldn't get out of the van to sit on a chair at the sidelines of the soccer field. I asked an official if we could drive the van onto the end of the grass, so Bill could see Benjamin play, and he said we could. Bill was so proud of Benjamin. He was perpetual motion, naturally athletic, and, despite his small size, he outran most of the kids, never seeming to tire. He had a strong kick, too! I still laugh when I remember the referee who picked him up by his belt as he just kept running in the air. It was hilarious! The day was very special. The other parents of the team members were all so kind and understanding. They were not only rooting for my child, but they were also rooting for our family. We felt the love. But things went downhill quickly after that soccer game.

By the time we got back to Mom and Dad's house, Bill was running a fever that kept climbing. I got him into a cool bath, but it wasn't helping. I put a call into our oncologist in North Carolina. We were so far from the Asheville hospital, and I didn't know whether to take a chance driving back. The doctor calmly and firmly told me to face it.

He said, "Bill is not going to pull out of this, Mrs. Stapleton. You need to prepare yourself."

He was kind and compassionate but very clear and firm with me. He went on to say he would handle the paperwork to transfer Bill's care to another doctor at the beach. Within days, we would be relocated at the beach and scheduled to go to a new oncologist at the local cancer center. There was still a part of me that refused to believe Bill wouldn't be healed. I clung to my belief that God had finally made a way for us all to be together again. I seriously think it was because I just couldn't let go of my *picture-perfect* ideal family. Wasn't it tragic enough we were missing a child? I still hadn't really let go of my dream to have a family photo with Will. I could not even begin to entertain the thought of a family portrait without a Dad.

XVIII

God's Pursuit

*"'For My thoughts are not your thoughts, nor are your ways
My ways,' says the Lord. 'For as the heavens are higher than
the earth, so are MY ways higher than your ways, and My
thoughts than your thoughts.'"*

Isaiah 55:8-9 (NKJV)

Our new doctor was young and handsome, appearing at first more like an actor from the soap opera *The Bold and the Beautiful*; yet after our initial conversations, it was obvious and encouraging to see that he was, indeed, deeply passionate about saving his patients. In further conversations, we would find out that his dad had died of cancer, and he was on a personal mission to find a cure for this heinous disease. He was intentional about doing all he could for Bill, even sending his blood samples to other countries globally to see if there was an experimental cure somewhere. Bill was offered a bone marrow transplant, which was fairly new technology at the time in 1997, but ultimately, Bill chose to turn it down when he realized, even if it were successful, it still gave him only a 25% chance of survival. The young, highly motivated doctor was very aggressive in his treatments. I went with Bill to every appointment, not only because I loved him, but we were in this together. It was a battle we would fight, unified in our efforts, against the insidious enemy: cancer.

I had also quickly realized that no one should go through an illness alone. Everyone needs an advocate and another set of ears. I would find it ironic when Bill and I would talk about what the doctor said after an appointment that so many times we would each hear different things. I also kept my own detailed files on Bill's disease in my own tote bag. It helped with so many treatments, medicines, doctors, and hospital stays.

To date, the cancer center at the beach was amazingly proactive in caring for the whole family. They seemed to seriously value the fact that when cancer is discovered in one person, it affects the dynamics of the whole family. One day as I was waiting for Bill during a treatment, I was summoned into a case worker's office. Bringing Bill's file folder, I thought she was going to ask me about Bill, but instead, she asked me how I was doing. I was stunned. I didn't even know they did that kind of thing; it really touched my heart that she genuinely cared. She went on to ask me how I was caring for the children and myself. In our conversation, I told her I had just moved a recliner into the small bedroom I shared with my daughter and stocked the nightstand beside it with my Bible and encouraging books, ensuring that I had a private place to run away.

She grinned and said, "You are going to be fine."

I knew in my heart that she was right, and it was wonderful to hear that affirmation from her. It didn't change the fact that I was tired, stretched, and very weary, but it encouraged me to keep doing what I was doing: caring for Bill, loving my family, and caring for myself, too.

Watching and seeing our two young children witness the deterioration of their father's body was a nightmare for me. If I could have protected them from the horror, I would have. I felt helpless. I felt like life was whirling out of control, and I had no power to stop it. I can only compare it to Space Mountain in Disney World, a roller coaster ride in the dark. Even though it has ups and downs, nothing can prepare one for the jerks to one's neck and head. I just wanted it to stop. I wanted to get off the rollercoaster. Instead of fighting it though, I only tried to keep life as *normal* (whatever that was) as I could.

Our lives invaded my parents' lives. Our mountain home was far too remote to handle Bill's special needs now. Bill's battle for his life took over my parents' back sunroom, overlooking a backyard that was framed by an undeveloped property of thick woods. It was private and cheerful. Bill liked having Ben play with a friend nearby, and it was not unusual to have a child operating the automatic lift chair. I knew Julie was sad and anxious, but Ben, so young, seemed to be taking it all in stride.

Then one day he looked at his dad sleeping in the hospital bed and slipping his hand into mine and looking up at me, he fearfully questioned, "Is Daddy a skeleton now?"

I took a long hard look at Bill as he slept, his body ravaged by the disease, laboring to breathe. Studying the devastation, I desperately wanted to scream at God! *What are You thinking? If You are going to heal him, do it! If he is going to die, then take him! STOP messing with the children!* But instead, I stood there, achingly silent, as my heart wrenched in protest about what my children had to witness. I could only hope to model for them a peace in knowing and trusting that God had the plan and that He would not give us more than we could bear. I pondered that the very fact that we were going through this experience meant that God had already equipped us for it even if we didn't realize it.

I would honestly reply to my young son, "I guess Daddy

Last family pictures with Bill. This was his final visit at our beloved Lake Junaluska.

does look like he is a skeleton, but he is not. Daddy is just very sick."

Now that we were back at the beach, I wanted to be doing more with my children and with my friends, but that was not happening. Our lives now revolved around doctor's appointments, treatments, medicines, and side effects. There was so little time for anything else; the isolation was stifling. One of the sweetest gifts I received from a dear group of ladies was that they actually brought their prayer group to me by meeting at my parents' house once a week. I eagerly looked forward to the morning they would come. It helped bring some sweetness into the bitter taste of the disease.

Mom and Dad were like the support staff in a docudrama. Mom was an amazing cook, and her castle was her kitchen, so I never desired or tried to invade her domain. She was content to oversee and prepare meals, and someone from our network of friends continually dropped by with something special to help with the load. Mom was always a *worker bee*, such a help, an extra set of hands with her practical way of jumping in and getting it done no matter what it was. Dad was a retired master electrician and was always being asked to troubleshoot by doing minor repairs for his friends and neighbors. For me, though, Dad was my spiritual rock, with his quiet presence of prayer. Dad always had a scripture or a Word for me, and it was truly a gift from God to be with them both after being separated by so many miles for most of the years of my marriage. They had seen Bill at his worst, so, even with our turbulent past, Mom and Dad had great acceptance and compassion for Bill. It was the supernatural kind that can only come from God. They were an amazing support staff. I felt their love with every kindness they offered. I will always be grateful for the faith-filled parents God gave me.

Everyone in the close-knit neighborhood was aware of our situation, and people from the church kept in constant touch. Over the next few months, we felt the love and care as people reached into our circumstances, even designing, and building an outdoor ramp for Bill's wheelchair. The door was always open and frequented by many dear visitors. Mail came from friends we had from all over, expressing concern, giving hope, and promising prayer. I still fight the feeling of inadequacy when it comes to returning gratitude and my inability to write thank you notes. Again, *paying it forward* is the only way I can deal with the swells of gratitude that overwhelm me when I think of all the people who touched, poured into, and invested in our lives.

Occasionally, Bill would have a little extra energy, and we would get to church. Cancer seemed to give us more to laugh at in human nature. I laugh to this day as I recall a well-meaning friend coming up to Bill's wheelchair. Bill sat there, thin, and gaunt, paralyzed on his left side, and bald from all the chemo.

Cheerfully, she said to Bill, "You look so good!"

He politely replied, "Thank you," but then, as I leaned over his shoulder to ask if he was ready to be pushed into the service, he quipped to me with his crooked smile, "You know, that's the same thing they say about the corpse in the casket!"

I just shook my head and smiled; he was so right! Then again, there was the fellow that came up to him and said how glad he was to see him because he thought he had already died! Sometimes we just had to laugh! People say very funny and sometimes foolish things when they don't know what to say. Joyce and John stayed close to us during this time, and during a simple phone call one day with Joyce, she asked me how she could be of help. I facetiously replied that everything was really being taken care of, but if she could grab a few hours of extra sleep for me, it would really help me out. Of course, I meant it to be light-hearted, but I was up with Bill most nights. The wee hours of the night were the darkest and hardest for him. He couldn't sleep; his fears would try and take over, and foreboding thoughts loomed bigger. He had meds to sleep, but they didn't always help because of his pain. I would try and help him focus on the hope we had; sometimes, I would read scripture or play music or put on a good movie, but I was also getting up early every day to get the kids to school. I was stretched beyond my limit.

Within a week, Joyce had organized volunteers to come at 11:00 p.m. and sit with Bill through the night, so I could get some sleep. She had instructed them not to even talk to me but to send me to bed and accompany Bill through the darkest hours of night. They would bring videos, books, and special foods they thought he might enjoy. They would leave by 6:00 the next morning. It was an amazing blessing! I still have those friends who recount how encouraging and special their times were with Bill.

Every day I would wake up wondering what was going to happen. *Is this the day he gets healed? Is this our last day together?* Then, one ordinary day, when the Hospice aide, who had come to bathe and shave Bill, had just left as I was returning from dropping the children off at school and walking three miles on the beach. It was my best time of the day -- the early morning. (I still love it best and usually accomplish everything I need to before noon.) Bill called to welcome me and ask how many sharks' teeth I had found on my walk.

Grinning and kissing him on his bald head, I placed them in his hand and said, "I found five this time!"

It was so wonderful to be able to drink in God's beauty early in the morning at the beach. I came back energized for the day. Bill closely examined the sharks' teeth, rolling them in his hand.

Then he looked at me and said, "Do you know why God is giving you these sharks' teeth every day?"

"You tell me; why?" I replied.

Bill seriously looked at me and said, "They symbolize all the pain and damage I caused you. You will never be attacked again; just by holding one in your hand, it will remind you that *'no weapon formed against you will prosper'* (Isaiah 54:17, NIV) and that God is Bigger." It was a treasured promise and moment that I will always hold close to my heart.

This walk throughout cancer was giving us opportunities to say all the things we needed to say to each other. Cancer became a walk of mercy and grace for us as we intentionally took the time to value every moment and each other. It wasn't always easy though. My competitive husband declared one day, "You know, Lin, either way I win. I'll be healed whether it is here or in Heaven. I win!"

I agreed, saying, "Yep! You win!" Inside, I knew whenever there is a winner, there is a loser, and deeper down, I was terrified. How were we going to make it without him? I had to believe even harder that he would be healed. I was still not willing to face the death sentence for Bill.

There were some stellar teaching moments, one of which was a morning when I returned from my daily walk on the beach. Bill wanted me to sit with him. I really had lots to do that day, and I wanted to get the laundry started. He was very weak and needing more attention. He became insistent, and I became resistant. We locked eyes as he patted the side of his bed. "Please, just sit here and be with me," he implored. I melted, remembering that was the very thing I had heard God say to me so many times when I would rush around with my lists and wear myself out *doing* all manner of things. I am so thankful that I listened to HIS small voice in me that day. We spent hours looking through our photo albums, laughing, and remembering the good days. We delighted in our children and the sweet memories, and I fully embraced the opportunity to be a *human being* instead of a *human doing*. All I needed to do sometimes was just *be* all present.

The only person Bill ever had contact with from his own family was his older brother, Bob, his wife Charlotte, and their two sons. They called and visited from New Jersey. It brought great peace to Bill, especially since he had been estranged from his parents for years and had carried a lot of emotional pain from his past. Even though He had worked through most of it with the copious amounts of counseling and therapy, I knew he was still troubled by his parents' unwillingness to come to see him. He worked at staying upbeat and positive for me and the children most of the time. But I know their rejection of him heavily weighed on him. We sincerely tried to make the most of every day, but again, in the darkness of those sleepless nights, he would find himself vulnerable to the enemy. Satan would play his insidious mind games to steal and destroy the peace and hope Bill had.

Bill painstakingly wrote a thirty-page letter to his parents. When he had finished, he gave me explicit instructions. I sent it off to them after I made one copy. I placed the copy in a sealed envelope just in case the children wanted to read it one day, and Bill made me swear that I would never leave the children with them. I promised him and did not question him further. They had never even met Benjamin, so it seemed a moot point. Truth be told, I have never bothered to read the whole letter, either.

With all the therapy Bill went through and the healing and deliverance he experienced, it was enough for me to hear him say to his brother, "The curse on us is broken. It will never be passed on."

Intuitively, I knew it had to do with the damage he had mentioned our last night at Lake Junaluska. I only needed to know that it was something devastating from his childhood. I believe I honor him by allowing it to be sealed and private.

Bill's health was declining rapidly. He had a hard time reconciling with the thoughts of leaving us. He would struggle with restless moments and dark thoughts through the night, but the steady, sweet visits of those faithful servants who came to sit with him brought God's light and kept the dark at bay.

Bill had gotten very close to our neighbor, Peggy, a retired entertainer. In a very special way, she became a *mother* to him. She was an unforgettable character -- brassy and sassy. She would tell us the most scandalous stories of her past, and sometimes, it seemed as though she was daring us to love her. We couldn't help but love her! She was in and out of the house every day usually dressed in outlandish night clothes. She spent many a night talking with Bill, saying she never slept anyway. She had a way of comforting Bill in his fears and making us all laugh at her outrageous antics. She brought some comic relief to the tragic circumstances we were living out. What a blessing she was to all of us!

I felt God's presence so powerfully in me and around us. It was like being in Holy Spirit school. I was learning to hear and follow His voice. Almost every morning, I would walk the water's edge. I would marvel at how I was all alone with God, but in a split second, my thoughts drowned out God's voice within the sound of the ocean. God was revealing to me that His voice was always speaking, never ceasing. As long as God was God, the ocean would speak with His voice. He was showing me that I had to make a conscious choice to listen for His voice. Much like tuning in to a favorite radio station, we must tune in to listen to God. My focus was being refined.

One day I was practicing this mental discipline by trying to rid myself of my own anxious thoughts when a jogger went by me with his ear buds in for his Walkman, revealing to me in that moment that many days I would come to the beach with my own agenda and things to do. I was at the right place to see and hear Him but not hearing a word that He was saying, let alone resting or walking in step and in peace with Him. The only way I would be able to receive the peace and rest of God was to still my mind and expect to receive with my heart. I would be more deliberate in meditation and practice His presence with a yearning heart. Soon, it was becoming my place to run to, rest, and recharge with Him. He would speak and I would hear. The seashore became my place of abiding with and learning to hear Him.

I also had to deal with facing the fact that it looked like Bill would not be healed here but would be going to Heaven to heal. Bill seemed to be in and out of consciousness. Often it seemed like he was bargaining with God to stay. I had been so afraid to make any plans because I felt that it was giving up, and I knew God could do anything. I felt like I should be gathering photos for a collage and possible funeral but felt paralyzed by the fear that God would think I had given up. Had I?

After expressing my fears to my registered nurse (RN) friend, Lynn, she asked, "Who says you have to change your plans?" It was an epiphany! Just because I made a plan did not mean I needed to keep it! Another layer of my control issues melting away! I was letting go and letting God be God. I worked on a possible funeral, not a probable funeral. I felt God's strength more and more these days, and I was learning to extend God's grace to myself.

XIX

God's Permission

"Who shall ascend into the hill of the LORD? Or who shall stand in his holy place? He that hath clean hands, and a pure heart; who hath not lifted up his soul unto vanity, nor sworn deceitfully. He shall receive the blessing from the LORD, and righteousness from the God of his salvation."

Psalm 24:3-5 (NIV)

I drove the kids to school on April 3, 1998, but did not go for my usual walk. Bill had been in a coma-like state for a week with no eating or fluids. He seemed to be hanging on as though something were left undone. During a sweet and intense time of prayer with dear friends, it became apparent through the Holy Spirit that Bill was struggling to leave. He was holding on to someone, and that someone was holding on to him. We all knew it was Julie. She had to release her daddy. The most heartbreaking factor in all of this was the children. Julie had such a bond with her dad, a powerful bond of love.

We had always said it was her prayers that went straight into the Throne room to heal our marriage and bring us back together as a family. Now, somehow, I had to help her understand that willingly releasing the person you love to be whom God wants them to be was the greater part of love. God gave up His only son, Jesus, to save us from our sin. Even though we didn't know God's bigger plan for her daddy, it looked as though his mission on this earth was coming to an end. She had to let him go back to God. Cancer had invaded and destroyed her daddy's *earth suit*, but her daddy would live on with Jesus in Heaven. One day, she would see him again, and we would understand it better. We'd all be together again.

I had talked and prayed with her the night before and cried silently as she went to her daddy's side in sheer obedience, gripping the rail of his bed with white knuckles. She shook from her head to her toes, desperately trying to let go of her daddy, the man she had wrapped around her little finger, the man who would dance with her whenever she asked, kiss her baby dolls on command, and let her stay up late and not tell Mommy. She found her inner strength to tell him *good-bye*. She told him that he could go and live with Jesus, and she promised him that she would be okay.

The next morning, I almost kept Julie home because of the emotional evening before, but she was up early and bravely facing school. She seemed relieved and peaceful. Both children kissed their dad good-bye, even though he hadn't responded for days. I took them to the school only ten minutes away and came straight home.

Bill had been under Hospice care the last three months. Our experienced Mercy Hospice RN was carefully monitoring Bill and seemed certain he would pass today. I was surprised when she asked me if she could have the honor of shaving and bathing him. Usually, it was the aide who did what the RN had asked to do. As I nodded permission, the nurse tenderly bathed and cared for Bill as he lay dying, saying that she had not bathed someone since nursing school but that she wanted to honor Bill in the only way she knew how. I stood by, tearfully watching her as she cared for him so tenderly. Bill's heart stopped two hours later, even though I already knew his spirit had left last night after his time with Julie. He was now with Will. Neither one of them would want to return. Instead, we who are left behind will be the ones that will dream of joining them one day.

I notified the school. The teachers and administration had all been so understanding and helpful during this stressful time. I went directly to each of the children's classrooms to collect them, and we left the school building quietly. Julie and Benjamin seemed to already know but didn't ask. I had planned to tell them that Daddy was gone as we walked on the beach. Plans suddenly changed as the gloomy sky darkened. A thunderstorm erupted overhead just as I parked at the beach access. The deluge of rain on the roof and windshield seemed to mirror and echo the pounding ache in our souls as we wept together in the minivan. Our hearts were breaking, and I desperately wished I could kiss away their pain and make it better as I told the children that Daddy was now with Jesus.

Grief is such a solitary thing that we all must do within ourselves. I could only pray that I would be able to help them navigate this part of their journey. I truly believe that when we lose someone we love, each of us grieves in the same measure that we have loved. The human soul longs for the love of a parent. Would my children grieve the rest of their lives? I could not shield my children from this sorrow. Instead, I had to trust that God was already present to comfort us and that He had a plan for us. Right now, we had Him and each other.

I felt left behind again. I longed to be with them in the glorious place I had once visited. I would dream about Will and

Bill reunited in the place where life sang! It seemed so much easier to give up in this life and go back to the amazing place I had been so many years earlier. I wanted to be in there again, where time was non-existent while love and light vibrantly reigned. But, deep within my soul, was an ember of hope and a new resolve with a determination that somehow, I would not let this loss defeat me. I promised God I would do all I could for my children, but I would not take a step without HIM leading us. I would wait on Him to lead us out of this *"valley of the shadow of death"* (Psalm 23). My babies had been through too much, and I vowed to Him that I would do everything I could to make sure they became healthy adults one day. Somehow, I had to trust that God would make every tear and heartache count.

I was weary emotionally and physically. I found myself begging God to give me strength to get through the next week with Bill's funeral in North Carolina and a memorial service back at the beach when we returned. He answered me with peace in my soul, and I felt Him carrying me again.

We arrived two days later at Lake Junaluska. It felt like coming home. My months with Shirley had been a respite compared to the strain of responsibility at the beach. As I look back, I see it now as a place like a watering hole in the desert, which God had provided to renew my strength for the rest of the journey. I admit that I spent too much time complaining about my separation from the children and was so grateful that God had stretched my faith and trust in Him as He built some rest into our cancer journey. We had experienced so much, and God had led so many people to come around us to help, encourage, and love us. I would be reticent to even put a list of names in print because of the likelihood of excluding someone. Only

God could have written this story with so many lives reaching out to us in kindness and compassion. Yet, even in a crowd of compassionate people, I was alone except for Him. He was my strength, and I felt Him carrying me. How could anyone but God really understand what was going on inside me as I braced for an uncertain future? Our savings were depleted after I paid for the funeral and headstone. Bill left no life insurance. How would I provide for my family? I longed for rest.

My strong, dear family converged at the Lake. Bill's service would be held the next day in Marion, North Carolina. Bill's parents never came, not even to see him one last time or to the funeral. They said they were sick. I felt just a small portion of the sting of rejection and betrayal that Bill must have felt during his whole life. My relief and knowledge that he was finally free and totally healed from all the pain he had carried was my solace.

The children and I said our good-byes to Daddy privately. As we looked at Bill's diseased ravaged body, I reminded the children that Daddy was alive in Heaven now, and we were just saying good-bye to his *earth suit*. Benjamin was just six years old and typically curious.

He was asking questions like, "Are his eyes still in there? Why is he so cold? Does he still have his legs?"

I did my best to answer each question, even dragging a nearby chair over to the casket, so Ben could climb up and see for himself. Julie just rolled her eyes and shook her head at Ben's comical behavior, and yet, it provided a sweet, poignant memory for our abbreviated family. Benjamin, just by being who he was, helped us both get through a most difficult time.

A few tears fell from Julie when I placed our pictures in his suit jacket pocket over his heart, but for the most part we were cried out. With a cancer journey, a lot of grieving is done by loved ones along the way, not just after the loved one passes away. We had talked about Heaven a lot. We read the book *Someday Heaven* by Larry Libby countless times together as a family over the past recent months. The children were as prepared as they could be and understood Bill was in Heaven, and his body was the *earth suit* that got a disease; now it needed to be buried.

I left the funeral service details up to Bill's students, friends, and colleagues. They put together a beautiful service of tribute for him. Many participated and honored Bill they knew. His colleague, Ed, even brought in a beautiful grand piano for the myriad of music played by some of his most accomplished students. It was sweet, sad, heartbreaking, joyous, and hope filled. Bill's love for music, talent, and his faith had been passed on to countless people in his lifetime. I felt as though he were watching. It was just what he would have wanted. We went from the funeral home to *Will's Hill* for the burial.

There was a deep relief that Bill was not suffering anymore, and I will admit to being a bit envious that he was living in the Land of Love with our beloved Will. Yep! He won! He got to be with Will first! I stood on the hill, standing next to a second opened grave and overlooking the panoramic beauty of the Cove. It seemed surreal that I was living the day that I had dreaded all these months. It was the same hill where Bill and I had stood and dreamed as young lovers. It was the same hill where I had shed so many tears while Julie had played, made countless daisy chains, and picked flowers for Will. The trees were alive with a new shade of green, and the March flowers were blooming in bunches on the hillside along with the new and uncertain season that was budding for my family. I still treasure the image in my mind of the silhouettes of father and son seated side by side on this hill in the twilight watching for the train to come around the bend. Now, two headstones stand side by side, both lives gone too soon. They are no longer here, but are in the next world, a more beautiful world without death and disease. A real place that I had briefly visited a long time ago.

Family and friends from far and near were gathered once again on the beautiful knoll in the Cove to say goodbye. It seemed supernatural, yet fitting, when at the end of the graveside service, the train, as if on cue, chugged through the crossing below as we all watched in amazement. Once again, blowing its resounding whistle, the train seemed to signal a journey to a new destination – a place beyond where we can go, a brilliant place where peace and joy reside, a place where one day we will all be together again.

I was still too afraid to think of the uncharted future that the children and I faced. There was no way I could look at the big picture ahead for me. Instead, I chose to continue to live the rhythm I had learned through the cancer, one moment at a time. I would not get ahead of Him. God gave me the strength to live by faith each day and not give in to my fears. I had been learning that God was not restricted by time. His timing was always perfect, even though He didn't wear a watch or use a calendar. It took all my mental and emotional energy not to worry or be anxious. The doctors had only given Bill a few months to live, and yet Bill fought each day to have one more day with his family. He made every moment count for God, and that gave us one scant year with him.

I made a deliberate choice not to let my imagination run away with me but to purposely meet each challenge as it came. I was learning that God gave me enough grace for each day and a refill each morning as the new day began. I would hold fast to Lamentations 3: 22-24. *"His compassions never fail. They are new every morning; great is Your faithfulness"* (NIV). I pictured a basket next to my bed, full to the brim with grace as I awoke, and by the time 10 p.m. came, I was *knocking on empty* with nothing left in me or in my basket. I would make myself go to bed, confident that it would be filled to the brim again in the morning, and I would make it through another day. The song we sang often in worship at this time was "God Will Make A Way" by Don Moen. It had a catchy tune, and I found the melody going over and over in my head. I slowed down one morning on the beach to really embrace and receive the simple truth of the message. God had carried me so far. I knew God would continue as the song said, "He will do something new today. . . . God will make a way."

The message of this song was so personal to me. He had led me all through the wilderness of the shadow of death. He had provided a never-ending flow of strength, support, and compassion all through the desert journey, and I knew He just wanted me to take Him at His Word. He cannot be heard if we are not still. I was learning to listen for His Spirit voice. I had heard His voice now many times, and I was accustomed to waiting in silence. I knew He was holding me close to Him and carrying me once again.

Summer of 1998 -- two headstones are now placed on the knoll overlooking the train tracks and beautiful Blue Ridge Mountains.

XX

God's Provision

"In the world you will have tribulation; but be of good cheer,
I have overcome the world."

John 16:33 (NIV)

"For it is God who works in you both to will and do His good
pleasure...children of God without fault in the midst of a
crooked and perverse generation, among whom you shine as
lights in the world."

Philippians 2:13-15 (ESV)

I have a vivid memory of myself as a painfully shy, awkward sixteen-year-old good girl. I was sitting in a church pew, along with a couple hundred other teenagers at a regional youth rally that many church youth groups attended. Frankly, I think most of us attended just to check out the boys from other churches, but nevertheless, I had just heard an amazing testimony by a young man slightly older than myself. He shared his gripping story of how he had been caught up in a lifestyle punctuated by tripping out on LSD, coupled with alcohol and promiscuity, since he had snuck his first drink from the bar in his own home. He testified how Jesus came into his life and miraculously delivered him, giving him direction and purpose in his life for the first time. As he finished his message, he had us bow our heads together in prayer. I had been inspired by the speaker and challenged to live a pure and clean life for God. I wanted to dedicate my whole heart and life to God, but in that moment, all I could do was complain to God because I wanted to give Him everything I had, and all I had to offer Him was my love and a boring testimony!

Up until that moment, all I had to say about my faith in Jesus was when I asked Him to come into my heart. I remembered it vividly: Five-year-old girl asks Jesus into her heart after listening to Bible Stories on records. The little girl knew she was a sinner and needed Jesus to pay for her sin because she had just carved her initials into her bedroom dresser with a paper clip. Her mother discovered it. When asked if she did it, the little girl lied and said her sister did it, but her little sister didn't even know how to write! The little girl knew she desperately needed Jesus. She knew she needed Him because she was a sinner. Her dad kneels with her in prayer and leads her through the sinner's prayer. She gets to stay up and tell her mom when she comes home. Yay! Young girl loves Jesus, and wants to serve Him, so she tries to obey Him and never sin again. *Lord Jesus, how will you ever use me when my testimony is SO boring! Boring!*

I hope you laughed at my naïve thought process. I still do. Major hint: <u>Never</u> complain to God! I left the meeting that night feeling useless to God. I had no idea of the arduous journey He had in store for me.

As I look back through my seasoned life today, I marvel at His love and patience with me as I stumbled through my journey complaining to Him. With all my railings and whining, questions and confusion, and too many hours spent on the pity-pot, I would always be slammed by the question of *Why does God allow evil? Why didn't God just get rid of Satan when he broke the rules in Heaven before the earth and people came to be? Why am I such a sinner?* The part that evil, disease, and death play in the world left me with countless questions. Put simply, I still wondered why I had damaged that piece of furniture. *Where does evil come from?*

I read many good books about the grief process, but the part where they brought me very little comfort or understanding was the piece of my story that warranted someone maliciously and deliberately wanting to impart evil to unsuspecting random persons. Intentional malice was the part of the murder trial that the prosecution had successfully proven. People die, accidents happen, and crime is everywhere, but when evil is indiscriminately meted out on random innocents, no one seems to be able to put any of the pieces back together. Even the steps through the grief process are random and unpredictable through homicidal trauma, not to mention the fact of deadly disease indiscriminately inflicted upon humanity from babies to the elderly. You see, I had continued to ask *Why?* That question is certainly indulged by God, but it is actually the wrong question to ask of a Sovereign. We might do better to ask God, "What are You teaching me?" or "What must I do next?"

After Will was murdered and my family seemed irreparable, my questions about God and Who He was rolled around in my head like a noisy rock tumbler. Over these years, God has lovingly and patiently endured my tantrums and tirades as I have searched His Word and felt His presence. It is still up to God, whether we believe in Him or not. HE is still in control, whether we like it or not. HE is Sovereign, whether we acknowledge Him or not. GOD IS BIGGER than anything we are going through. We act out instead of believing that God has it all under control, and He is working it all for our good. We blame those around us and rationalize and justify our unhealthy behavior.

He is returning for His bride very soon. That is why He sent me back. I had no idea those many years ago who I was to Him. I did not know that I was dearly loved, chosen, holy, blessed, blameless, redeemed, and forgiven before I ever was born. I based my relationship with God on my less than perfect performance and let that build a wall of fear around my heart. I put myself in a prison of guilt and shame as I held tightly to my wrongs instead of accepting His free *get out of jail card*.

His plan for the wedding of the ages is totally in the hands of the wedding planner of all time. The venue for the full banquet is set; Jesus has it all paid for and ready to go. As His bride, we must be preparing for the Groom's return and our thoughts filled with loving the Groom with all our heart, soul, mind, and strength -- to love others as we love ourselves in the light of His love. We do not need to be concerned with any details of the wedding. Instead, we need to simply be *in love* with the Lover of our souls, the One True Holy Living God. We need to know how loved we are and receive the love He has lavished on us. We will never feel His love if we do not read the love letters in HIS *planner* and quiet our souls to spend time with Him.

On one wall of my vaulted, ceilinged living room hangs an exquisite Belgium tapestry. It is the closest picture I have found to replicate the temple area in my trip to Heaven. It shows a stunningly beautiful temple courtyard on the shores of Lake Como in Italy not far from the simple village my Grandfather Toro immigrated from many years ago. When I first saw a picture of the woven tapestry on *eBay*, I knew I had to have it! I didn't want to risk losing it, so I called my good friend, Bob, who loves the bidding wars on *eBay*, and I asked him to get it for me (we all have our talents). Bob won me the steal of the century! I knew we took a chance; all the description had said was that it was a 5x6 "rug." It arrived rolled up in a vacuum cleaner box, and what I took out of the reused packaging was an authenticated and numbered, perfectly gorgeous and valuable tapestry! I joyfully hung my priceless gift from Heaven!

Daily I look at that tapestry in its intricately woven threads of blue-green water, hills and mountains, and prolific flowers. There is one very important detail about the colors though: They are not at all vibrant and alive like I saw in Heaven. All the colors in my tapestry are rich but softly muted shades of color. There is no living light source, only reflected light. Gently, by its mere understated presence, it reminds me of my unforgettable trip to the other side of life.

Here I am, one ordinary person, one grain of sand on the beach, living in this magnificent world created by a spoken Word from the voice of God. Yet, like every other person in the world, I am touched by darkness, death, and brokenness. Right now, I am living in the muted colors of the *underside* in my tapestry where the threads are a jumble of confusion, where everyone has an expiration date, and where all our lives come preprogrammed with the shadow of death. Our fragile, and temporary *earth suit* will be absorbed into this planet one day. Yet, the most real part of me is my soul, made vibrant and alive through Jesus's resurrection! My mind, my will, and my emotions went to Heaven that day long ago. Somehow, I was supernaturally transported by the powerful energy source of God's Holy Spirit. The only way back to our Creator is still through partnering with God in the death of His only Son, Jesus. Jesus told us *"I am the way, the truth and the life; no man can come to the Father except by Me"* (John 14:6, NIV). He so wants us all to know that HE IS BIGGER! He has always had the plan!

He wants our love. He wants us to be in love with Him with every fiber of our being. He will not compete with another grain of sand or the other things this world offers. He wants to be our greatest love. When He is given His rightful place in our lives as the true lover of our souls, the other relationships fall into place. Every time I see Him or sense Him, or hear from Him, I have immediate access to Him in His throne room -- now. My soul has been made alive in Him!

I have endured and been found faithful. I have truly learned, some may say, the hard way, but they would say that about Job, too. Nevertheless, I have learned who I am and how loved and precious I am to Him! I have also learned a lot about who I am not. I cannot ever do God's job. That job can still only be done by an all-seeing, all-knowing, always present Sovereign. I have learned I am no longer a victim and not merely a survivor; I am an *overcomer*! There are other over-comers in this world, many sit in Veterans Administrative hospitals, nursing homes, and wheelchairs. Too many sit silently, not ever being able to share their stories, but radiating with the "peace that passes all understanding," an indomitable joy, gratitude, and love for others. I have written out my story for them. I hope to encourage or inspire them to never, ever, ever give up, whatever your circumstances may be. God knows us better than we know ourselves. The angels watch us and marvel at what we endure through Him and their love for God is encouraged.

For now, I wait. There are still those days that I wish I were on the other side, but I know I was sent back here to tell others of the mystery of God. As the Apostle Paul wrote in his letter to the church in Ephesus,

> *The mystery is that people who have never heard of God and those who have heard of Him all their lives (what I have been calling outsiders and insiders) stand on the same ground before God. They get the same offer, the same help, and same promises in Christ Jesus. The Message is accessible and welcoming to everyone, across the board.* (Ephesians 3: 5-6, NIV)

God writes a different challenge and story on every life. Our mission on this side of eternity is to live it in the Divine Light of His Word, guidance, and strength. As Paul continues to write in the letter in Ephesians,

> *You were all called to travel on the same road and in the same direction, so stay together, both outwardly and inwardly. You have one Master, one faith, one baptism, one God and Father of all, who rules over all, works through all, and is present in all. Everything you are and think and do is permeated with Oneness. But that doesn't mean you should all look and speak and act the same. Out of the generosity of Christ, each of us is given his own gift.* (Ephesians 4:4-7 MSG)

We take our lead from Christ, who is the source of everything we do. He keeps us in step with each other. His very breath and blood flow through us, nourishing us so that we will grow up healthy in God, robust in love. (Ephesians 4: 16, MSG)

When we live as overcomers in this world, we make a bold statement to the enemy, Satan and his realm of darkness. Our lives demonstrate that he is still a LOSER! We also energize the Spirit World in Heaven when the angels see and marvel what we can endure in this life and still trust in Him without seeing Him. We overcome evil when we choose to be better instead of bitter, and when we choose to thank Him for our lives instead of griping about our circumstances. GOD IS BIGGER! God does it all through flawed, weakened human vessels, vessels that can only function in His strength, human vessels that have fully surrendered to Him.

A believer trusts that when he/she is weak, God becomes his/her strength. The greatest battle for humanity was won the day that Jesus rose from the grave and is seated now with His Father in the Throne Room. He overcame torture and death for us, and He assures us that we are His and He is ours with every breath that we take when we share in His suffering and turn to Him for comfort and healing. One can run, rebel, complain, act out, try alternative methods to deal with one's pain, but His message is still the same, and ultimately, HE Wins!

XXI

God's Providence

"If you do what the LORD wants, he will make certain each step you take is sure. The LORD will hold your hand, and if you stumble, you still won't fall. As long as I can remember, good people have never been left helpless, and their children have never gone begging for food. They gladly give and lend, and their children turn out good."

Psalm.37:23-26 (CEV)

It is only by looking back on events that you realize that there were some decisions made in crucial times that turned out with amazing results. I guess I am trying to say the same thing as *Hindsight is always 20-20.*

Bill and I had been married twenty-five years. We had made many mistakes as I am sure the LORD knew we would. But one thing we had grown in as the years moved us forward was "living by faith and not by sight." We knew we were not just survivors, but we were over comers! When Bill was dying, he would often say, "Even if I die, I win!" Yes, to have that assurance of Heaven having a reservation waiting for you was wonderful. Even though I would agree outwardly, I would also think to myself, *But I will be left behind, and I'm scared.* I knew that if I looked too closely at my current circumstances, I would be terrified. But I was beginning to catch the bigger view, the vision that God was going in front of me, making a way for me and my babies, even as we slept.

As a young widow now, my circumstances looked so bleak. Yet it was even more terrifying to entertain the thought that God would not take care of me. At this point in my life, I had buried a young child to murder and was still standing. I had walked through the *"Valley of the shadow of Death"* (Psalm 23), burying my life mate to disease. I was deeply scarred and wounded now that I was left behind by my husband and provider; I felt like I had been sucker-punched and deserted. However, this time I could not afford the time to sit on my *pity-pot*.

The brunt of my family's future weighed heavily on me. I would soak in the insightful words of the Prophet Isaiah in Chapter 54. God began to breathe life back into me through His words. Gradually, the ever-strengthening words of "Your Maker is your husband, the Lord Almighty is His name" rang louder than the voice that wanted to tell me I was all alone and helpless. I knew it was the voice of the accuser trying to take me down. He was not going to steal my peace or joy anymore! I would read the passage of scripture over and over and God would tattoo it onto my mind and heart and into my soul. Many times, over the years in God's Word, I have replaced the general personal pronouns to reflect God speaking directly to me.

Allow me to share it the way I read Isaiah 54 nearly every day that first year without Bill:

> *Do not be afraid; Linda, you will not be put to shame. Do not fear disgrace; you will not be humiliated. You will forget the shame of your youth and remember no more the reproach of* **your** *widowhood. For your Maker is your*

husband – the LORD *Almighty is his name -- the Holy One of Israel is your Redeemer; he is called the God of all the earth. The* LORD *has called Linda back, a wife deserted and distressed in spirit -- a wife who married young, only to be rejected," says her God. "For a brief moment I abandoned Linda, but with deep compassion I will bring her back. In a surge of anger HE hid His face from her for a moment, but with everlasting kindness He will have compassion on Linda, says the* LORD *her Redeemer. To me this is like the days of Noah, when I swore that the waters of Noah would never again cover the earth. So now I have sworn not to be angry with Linda, never to rebuke her again. Though the mountains be shaken and the hills be removed, yet my unfailing love for Linda will not be shaken nor my covenant of peace be removed, says the* LORD, *who has compassion on her. "O Afflicted city, lashed by storms and not comforted, I will rebuild Linda with stones of turquoise, her foundations with lapis lazuli. I will make her battlements of rubies, her gates of sparkling jewels, and all her walls of precious stones. Linda's children will be taught by the* LORD, *and great will be their peace. In righteousness she will be established: Tyranny will be far from her; Linda will have nothing to fear. Terror will be far removed; it will not come near her. If anyone does attack Linda, it will not be my doing; whoever attacks her will surrender to her. See, it is I who created the blacksmith who fans the coals into flame and forges a weapon fit for its work. And it is I who have created the destroyer to wreak havoc; no weapon forged against Linda will prevail, and she will refute every tongue that accuses her. This is the heritage of the servants of the LORD, and this is Linda's vindication from me, declares the LORD.*

In Isaiah 54:11, the meaning of the Hebrew for this word afflicted is uncertain. This reference will also explain why I began to wear turquoise and pearl jewelry as a tangible and continual reminder that I have been rebuilt and transformed by the very hands of God. I chose to believe and trust God's words for me! This was my vindication! I felt free and clean! It was a new day! I saw myself in the God breathed Words delivered through His prophet Isaiah for His beloved Israel. These were encouraging Words, spoken so long ago, yet just as relevant today for me in a very personal way. What a Glorious God! It was like being caught in a torrential downpour of His blessing, freedom from my past, and promise for my future; God soaked me with His Words!

Two months had passed since Bill's funeral. Pastor Greg came up to me and asked me if I would share my testimony of God's faithfulness to me. I told him that I would but that it would probably be too long. He said not to worry; they would find a way to condense it. As I left the church, I was reminded of a Great Commission video Bill, and I had done. But with all our moves, I had no idea where it was. I told God if HE wanted me to do as they asked, He would have to direct me to the video. The next day, I went to the storage unit filled with the boxes and stuff of the past twenty-five years. I had no idea of where to start, but as you might have guessed, it was right on top of the first box I opened! We had only asked for one copy as payment for doing it, and God placed it right in front of me. No one had even played it since 1987.

I handed it off to the pastoral team with the full confidence that it was time for me to speak again. The video gave all the background for Will's murder, and I would just have to speak of God's faithfulness through the cancer. Even now I marvel at the favor God showered on me as I spoke that first time after so much heartbreak. With my knees shaking and heart pounding, the video clip of the essentials of the murder and my personal message of God's forgiveness and His faithfulness to my family was spoken. As the whole congregation stood in ovation for God, I knew that from that day forward I would proclaim God's Sovereignty and His goodness as long as I had breath in my body. He had written His story onto my life, and I would be faithful to proclaim it. This was a new beginning for the rest of my life. I was resolved to take "My Maker" at His Word and trust Him to be the Lover of my soul, Father to my Fatherless children, and provider for my family. Oh yes, I would have to do my part, and I was more than willing. We would shakily start a new beginning as an abbreviated family, not the *picture-perfect* stock family photo, but we were what we were, it was what it was, and we had each other.

For a woman, experts agree that her most basic need is to feel secure, and whatever she needs to feel secure she will pursue. I had never realized until this time in my life how much I had depended on Bill to provide. I not only depended on him for the creature comforts of life, but the security that comes with provision. Without money coming in, I was terrified. I could understand the fear firsthand of why women start looking for a man with a paycheck with whom to start over.

Even well-meaning friends said, "Linda, your children need a father, and you need someone who will love you and provide for your family." Though I understood why they would say that, I knew deep in my soul that God had promised to carry me and walk with me as our new season of life began. I reasoned that if it were what God wanted for me, then He would make it happen. Meanwhile, I had to stay focused on getting a job and helping my children heal. God would provide a part-time receptionist job, which still gave me the time the children needed with me. I sensed something else was coming; I just didn't know what it was. For the time being, it was perfect. I gave myself at least a year to heal and before I would make any big decisions.

I know that if I were reading my story, I would be looking forward to a sweet storybook ending starring a strong Christian man waiting somewhere in the future. It would be the story of a great guy who loved and trusted God. His story would be one of how God prepared him for me and my children. It would bring you a measure of peace, knowing I was cared for, provided for, and most of all loved and not alone. And yet as inviting as that may sound, I knew God was still refining and renewing my life, as well as rebuilding and recalibrating my family. I knew that I would not try to make anything happen. I knew that *"My Maker was my husband; the Lord Almighty was His name"* (Isaiah 54:5). I knew He could make all things new and I only wanted what He wanted for my family.

"Pepsi-Nana" was our beloved family member -- constant companion and comforter. She lived until 2000 at the dog age of 91. She was faithful, loyal, and true.

We have so many precious memories with my parents.

Charles E. Toro: June 29, 1925 - May 26, 2003
Sarah (Sally) Toro: May 30, 1927 - April 26, 2018

Christmas with Mom and Dad.
Left to Right:
Julie, Mom, Ben, Dad, and Linda.

XXII

God is Praiseworthy

"Every good and perfect gift is from above, from the Father of light and the Lord of love."

James 1:17 (KJV)

I was still receiving the small amount of mission support money that our church gave us monthly. Since Bill was now gone and the circumstances changed, I went to the church administrator to see what they were going to do. I knew that even though it was not a lot, we needed it, but I was also willing to work for it. Our church at that time ran a counseling center next door to the administrative offices. Nearing the end of the training in Alabama when cancer had been discovered, I knew counseling was what I was gifted and called to do; despite lack of formal credentials at that time, my experience, innate insight, and spiritual gift of wisdom allowed me to eventually become sought after for spiritual guidance and counsel. I came on staff in the administrative offices when their administrative assistant left on maternity leave, and my children started back to school. I could also use my time at the office to counsel people next door at the center. The church was willing to allow flexibility within my schedule and the kid's school schedule around my hours. It was a perfect fit!

Bill had died without leaving any life insurance; the minivan was paid for, and the only debt I had was Bill's medical bill. It was a mountain, but I was determined to pay a small amount each month for the rest of our lives. I was most grateful for the gift of starting over and the priceless treasure of my children. Even they would dance around the day I received an unexpected phone call from the cancer center that cancelled all the debt. I still don't know *how* the $150,000 hospital bill was settled; I just know I got a call from the Medical Center's Collections Department, notifying me that the account balance was *paid in full*. That was the first of many miracles the kids and I would begin to experience

My parents' days of raising their children were behind them, but they provided solid roots of love and a secure roof for my small, fragile family. It was tight living in their small bungalow, but we trusted the *Father to the fatherless* and the *Lover of my soul* to provide. Increasingly, over the past years in the mountains, I had longed to be closer to my parents. I could never have foreseen this, but it was a definite answer to that prayer. God had made a way. I will always be grateful for their unselfish love and compassion. Over the next year, through God's supernatural network of compassionate friends and the generosity of people, an addition was built on to my parents' modest retirement home.

Building an addition was birthed over lunch one day with my friend, Vicki, when we talked about the possibility of adding on to my parents' house. With her background in design and a can-do spirit, she then proceeded to draw a sketch on a napkin of what an extra bedroom, bath, closet, and entry way would look like. I took that napkin and a tablet of graph paper and took measurements when I got home and asked God to provide. It was the beginning of a movement within the Christian Community. I became an independent contractor of sorts, and soon, everything from the zoning office, concrete slab, and plumbing fell into place. Dad did all the electrical wiring, and we even included an attic for storage.

A building contractor voluntarily came all the way from New Jersey and framed the whole addition in one weekend, so when the drywall guys hung the walls and asked, "Who framed this?"

I held my breath and asked, "Why do you ask?"

The fellow replied, "Rarely do we find such perfect corners!"

Yea God! He was even giving us His best! Most everything was gifted or at basic cost. What was done for my family was done years before the world had even heard of *Extreme Makeovers*! That first year God would clearly make a way and a place for us to rebuild and heal as a family.

I refused to get ahead of God with my future. I knew He had me in the palm of His hand, and I just wanted to do what He asked of me. I knew He was carrying me, and I knew He was asking me to continue to live as we had been, one moment at a time. That way I wouldn't miss His plan for me and the children. I used to even carry a laminated *Family Circus* cartoon in my Bible that said, "Today is a gift – that's why they call it a present." I was determined to keep walking the beach and "living by faith and not by sight." Every day He was my first thought in the morning and my last thought at night. I treasured my early mornings with Him to get through the day.

Right after the addition was built, Peggy, our neighbor from across the street, called me over to her house and took me into her spare room. In the corner, was a beautiful, tufted velvet chaise. She pointed to it and said, "I want you to have this in your bedroom for your *God-time*. As crude and rough as she acted, she never missed anything or an opportunity to give. I joyfully accepted the beautiful treasure! Our lives have been open books for all to see, and even she saw what was most important to me.

In reflection of these years, I will always remember being impacted by a testimony that an elder of our church gave. He was a dignified young father with a beautiful wife and family, a successful businessman, and was respected by all. I was sitting near the front and was a bit surprised at how nervous he seemed as he clutched what I assumed was his Bible. He went on to share how he had always struggled with anxiety and inadequacy even to the point of feeling physically sick. Then he shared that when he got serious about his relationship with God and let Jesus take over his life, everything began to change. He then opened the leather book he was carrying, and what he showed us was his day planner. Intentional time with Jesus and meditation, prayer or study, was prioritized and ordered his life instead of his circumstances. It inspired and affirmed me!

Over the years, there rarely has been a day when I didn't kneel before my Lord with an open day planner and my Bible side by side. I have trusted Him to order my steps and keep us going in the right direction. It still makes me laugh when I remember one early morning, I could hear the children moving around and getting ready for school when I heard a loud patter of running feet, and Benjamin burst open my bedroom's French doors. Breathlessly he yelled, "Excuse me God! Mom! The toilet is overflowing!" As I reflected later, on his interruption and outburst, I just had to laugh at his good manners and acknowledgment that God was there. What joy there is in His presence! Those closest to you know *real* when they experience it.

XXIII

God's Practical Plan

"Follow my example as I follow the example of Christ."

1 Corinthians 11:1 (KJV)

Benjamin became my immediate and greatest concern after Bill's death. I had been pulling out clothes to get ready for the impending school year when I started to notice his pant legs' length. I somberly realized that he had hardly grown. I put long pants on him that he had worn two years before, and they were still fine. I quickly got him in to see the pediatrician, realizing that both children had been neglected in this area of regular physical check-ups. We were living in the South where even the winters are mild, and Ben's preference was always shorts and sneakers. But truth be told, cancer had consumed our lives, and we were still digging our way out. I was horrified, feeling like I had failed to care for my children while tending to Bill, but I also determined in that moment that my children had to become my first priority.

Benjamin, six, seemed healthy and very active but somewhat detached and in his own little world of play. His grief counselor assured me that children grieve in their own way and with their own timetable, but I was still left with the pressing question, "Why wasn't Benjamin growing?" Every living thing has growth built into it, right?

At the recommendation of our pediatrician, I took

Benjamin to a pediatric endocrinologist at MUSC (Medical University of South Carolina). The hospital was two hours away, so every time we went, I was determined to build some fun into it. It became our special time together, so we took his fishing pole, Frisbee, balls, and usually packed a picnic. He loved casting his Mickey Mouse fishing rod off the Battery in Charleston.

The doctors started a base line for his growth by taking x-rays of the growth plate in his wrist along with regular visits, a myriad of tests, evaluations, and counseling for nutrition. That next year he grew one-fourth of an inch, barely making the growth chart. I knew he wasn't thriving, but I did not know what else to do. In some ways he just wasn't checked into life. What had happened to my independent trailblazer? Where had the little boy who fearlessly entered school gone? I made the decision with lots of prayer for Benjamin to repeat Kindergarten, hoping it would give him some time to emotionally recalibrate. After all, what he really wanted to do was play. For the most part, holding him back that year was a decision I have never regretted.

Julie, on the other hand, was thriving with a teacher she adored and a sweet group of friends and classmates, as well as immersed in dance classes at the studio. God truly knew I could not handle one more thing. I was personally struggling with the new label of *widow*. I knew I was more than qualified for my new identity, but my life seemed incongruous with my expectation of widowhood. My actual life was so full of activity with the children, overseeing the addition, and my work that I truly just felt like a *single mom* with no child support money. I really didn't have the time to reflect much about my position or label in this world, so I just tried to embrace this new life for my family, trusting that we would survive. My faith and trust would be stretched but deepened. It still was one day at a time and many times one moment at a time.

The first year flew by but with its end came a personal challenge for me. There was no shortage of *good* Christian men looking for a *good* Christian woman in our large vibrant church. I distinctly remember a friend asking me if I would at least be willing to go out with a good friend of hers. I still felt *very* married inside and with such young children; young children who had just witnessed the horrific trauma of watching their dad painfully deteriorate in front of them. I decided to ask Julie, now twelve, what she thought about maybe Mom going out on a date. Her response was *politically correct*, "We only want you to be happy, Mom," but to my horror, I saw her bravely trying to ignore the tears that filled her eyes but never fell. Obviously, it still wasn't time. We all needed to heal, and that would take lots of Jesus and a lot more time.

It would have been so easy to isolate. I felt like I really didn't *fit* anywhere in this world. But the truth is I forged ahead, knowing and believing that we needed to be surrounded by community. With young children having homework and activities, I knew I could not be gone from them a lot. We had spent too much time separated by the circumstances of our lives. They needed the security of my presence and the emotional investment only a parent can give. So, I began to teach and host a Bible study group out of our home once a week. That way, others came to us, and I didn't need childcare. It provided my children with an extension of people who were interested in growing closer to God and experiencing God in practical ways. Mom and Dad loved it, too, and God used our hospitality to weave us into a wonderful body of believers. It also brought order and purpose to our home, knowing we would have company every week.

As I look back on that season of life though, I know it was my deliberate conscious decision NOT to try to be their dad that brought me the most peace and strength. It took a lot of the burden off. I took God's Word and held it up to Him, especially the verses that said that He will be the "Father to the fatherless" and the husband to the widow or the woman rejected. The promises of Isaiah 54 buoyed and cradled me like a life raft out in the rough, turbulent waters. I told my children that I knew I could not be their father, but I could be the best mother I could be. God was going to help me. I had a tenacious grip on God. Every man paled in comparison to what my Lord was for me. His Word was "better than life"; it was my comfort, my strength, and my song. I was surrounded by an encouraging church family and friends. I felt His presence with me, and my soul was touched and nourished in every sunrise on the beach, flower, smile, breeze, and hug. I saw and felt Him everywhere. When I was weak, He made me strong. I knew He was carrying me and would never let me down.

XXIV

God's Providence

God is so real to me; I want my children to have my same peace, too. So, I asked everyone I knew that were praying for Julie and Ben, to pray that Benjamin especially would start to see and understand that God was his Heavenly Father. I would often sit with the children at bedtime and remind them how their dad would elbow his way through the crowd of other proud parents so that he could get the best photos front and center when there was an awards assembly, recital, or ball game. We laughed at how her dad's behavior had sometimes embarrassed Julie but made her feel special at the same time. I would remind them that their Heavenly Father is always going to go *over and above* for them much like their dad did because God is totally responsible for them now that their dad was in Heaven. God would be able to do even more amazing things than their dad could, and besides, their dad was probably pushing his way into the Throne Room to make sure HE did! I know I embellished the picture, but hey, these are my babies. I desperately wanted them to be healthy. I honestly couldn't ever know how much of that took root, but it helped me let God be God and relax in the weight of my responsibility to be the sole nurturer, provider, and go-to person.

Benjamin still wasn't growing. In fact, he was barely on the standard growth chart. We were adding extra calories to everything with slices of cheese, slathering peanut butter on both sides of the sandwich, and feeding Ben constantly.

I barely smiled when he looked up at me one day and seriously said, "No more ice cream, Mom, please?"

Granpa and his *Vita Mix* though, cheerfully made Ben nutritious shakes. There were shakes of all colors (mostly green) and flavors usually masked by a banana, so nutritious that no one really wanted to know what was in them. Benjamin was the only one who chugged them down with no questions. It became their *guy thing* to do. By this point in time, a lot of serious conditions, too scary for me to talk about, had been ruled out over the past months, but we still had no real answers. Ben was seven now and in first grade. His Heavenly Father had provided a full scholarship for him in a private Christian school. One was generously offered to Julie, as well, but she chose to stay in public school.

I treasured the time we had in the car every day. It was time to talk or work on spelling words, and some of my sweetest memories had happened in our minivan.

One day on our way to school and work, God gave us an incredible gift. Benjamin, who always rode *shotgun* (again, before airbags became standard) casually said to me, "Mom, do you know that God has two different arms?"

The question took a minute to register in my brain, and frankly, I laughed at his apparent creativity, and then I stopped because I realized I was receiving the answer to my prayer. I had been boldly asking God to show Benjamin that God was his real

Father! I pulled over to the side of the street to process Ben's declaration.

I asked Ben, "Tell me what they look like?"

He replied in detail of how God's arms had really big muscles, even demonstrating with his hands the approximate size and that God's right arm was the arm that reached down and helped him hit the T-ball out into the *green grass*! I had been surprised during t-ball season that very few of the boys could hit the ball into the outfield, but Ben was consistently a crowd-pleaser as the other parents called him *mighty Ben*! Wow!

I could not hold back the tears of joy and relief to the fact that Benjamin had experienced a picture / vision from his Heavenly Father. It was somewhat natural to me since God had supernaturally done the same for me many times before. I hugged Ben and told him how happy I was that he had seen God. (We still had to get him to school though.)

While straightening myself and starting to shift the minivan into *drive*, Ben's cute young voice asked, "Mom, do you want to know what God's other arm looks like?"

I stammered, "Of course I do," as I shifted the minivan lever back into *park*. There was holiness in that minivan, and I needed to calm my spirit down to soak in it. I took a deep breath to focus myself as Ben looked directly into my soul with his *blue as the ocean* eyes framed by dreamy long lashes and said, "His other arm is just like yours, Mom. That's the one that holds me when I am sick and when I am sad – even His hand has fingernails like yours."

Oh, what joy flooded into my soul! Through my precious little boy, the Holy Spirit ushered in a peace beyond my understanding that day. In the future when I would default to worrying, I would make myself remember who Ben's dad really is! A God of might and power, but also love and comfort -- **the One True Holy Living God – Abba Father!**

Each time I relay Benjamin's vision, I am overwhelmed by God's intense love that He has for my storm-tossed family. God gave a picture of Himself that day to a little boy and his mother who, while going through the motions of life, desperately needed His supernatural touch. I know there are many others who need to know this, too. His amazing love and supernatural strength have carried us through these many years. For me, it will always be the most beautiful and complete picture of the true nature of God -- loving strength and loving comfort -- as He wrapped my fractured little family up in His arms and loved us as His own.

Benjamin would still have issues with growth for the next few years, showing very minimal growth until it came out in counseling that he equated growth with dying. He did **not want** to grow up because in his limited understanding, that meant he would die, too! Gripped by fear of dying, he had been refusing to grow inside his soul; talk about being strong willed! It was akin to *failure to thrive* that happens in infants. Armed with this new knowledge, we were able to help Ben process his thinking, and we stood on the scripture verse in Luke 2:52, *That (Benjamin would) grow like Jesus, in wisdom, stature and in favor with God and man.* We prayed it every night in bedtime prayers and better yet, trusted it. By the time Ben approached puberty, he chose not to do the growth shots; instead, he trusted God. We were pleasantly surprised in puberty, when, of all things, a snow board accident of a fractured wrist presented itself. A fresh x-ray revealed that he had a lot more growing to do in the growth plate, which the fracture had narrowly missed! He has grown steadily since, and today you would never guess that he ever had a problem with growth.

We were able to move out of Mom and Dad's home by the time Julie was approaching high school. It was time to sell the land, as well as, to part with the past. I had tried to hold onto the homestead in the mountains for my children. But financially I couldn't do it any longer. Our (Bill's and my) dream would have been to provide it as our children's inheritance, but God was clearly helping me to hold loosely the things of this world. The Ellis family had graciously looked after the acreage for me in honor of their close friendship with our family, but it was too much for me to hold on to. It was time, yes, time to sell the beloved acreage. The small cemetery where Bill and Will are buried was deeded out of our land for the whole community, so that remains a special place for me to return to. I still visit that beautiful spot in the mountains as I reflect and remember that season of my life and God's relentless faithfulness to my family.

Without the burden of the land in North Carolina, the beach was our home now. We were able to afford a modest home with a huge live oak in the back yard that Ben would climb and jump down into his trampoline. Ben picked the neighborhood because his best friend, David, lived there. I loved it because I knew God made it happen, and it was right for us, same great schools, close to the beach, and just five minutes away from Mom and Dad. During that same year though, Dad died after complications with surgery. Dad loved our Lord so much; he was rarely seen without his large-print Bible. Dad was seventy-six when he left us, but I will always remember what he said on his seventieth birthday.

He looked at me and said with all sincerity, "I can go now.

Seventy years is a full lifetime; it is how long King David lived, and anything extra is a bonus."

We buried his Bible with him, in fact, the cover was completely covered in duct tape, the silver kind though; it was before duct tape became fashionable. We also were able to give his fourteen other Bibles to each of the grandchildren. Dad's love of God's Word was his legacy to me. I don't want to live a day without it either.

My beloved *deposits* in Heaven were adding up. My truest gift and solace are that I got to spend Dad's last five years on earth near him. Momma, after being married fifty years, became a widow, too, and every day for the next fifteen years, I had the precious gift of my devoted mother.

The years blur together now. There were so many ways that God literally provided all our needs. Julie has often said that one of her goals when she grew up was to write all her Mom's *God Stories*. Over these years, He has proved Himself to be an amazing provider and husband. Even though I never really aspired to be anything but a wife and mother, He carved out a path for me to use my gift of wisdom through teaching, counseling, and mentoring. Obviously, the story HE has written on my life required a little more, and I was an eager learner.

I believe the ground is level at the foot of the cross. What I mean by that is that no one is greater or lesser in God's eyes. Pain and suffering are the common denominator no matter where you live in this world, no matter what you do, or where you come from. It is deep, real, and it is relevant to life. All people matter to God especially when they are in pain. In the Western world, the deep psychological pain of loneliness, abandonment, betrayal, and loss is as real as the pain of starvation, disease, and death in third world countries. All of humanity has the invitation from their Creator to look toward the One who made them and knows them best. We can use our pain and suffering to become more like Jesus. When we share and identify with His pain, we then share in the agony of the cross. We can embrace it and find peace in knowing the battle was won there, and one day we will be with Him. Or we can let bitterness invade and grow in our hearts that will only serve to distance us from our Creator and Savior. God is the only perfect judge. He knows us better than we know ourselves. He knows the past of every perpetrator of evil and died for them, too. God has made the way.

God made a way for me to nurture and raise my children, my priority, through the close-knit encouraging network of believers throughout the Beach Community. We don't all go to the same church building on Sundays, but we are bound heart to heart through Jesus Christ. I still love working these many years for Myrtle Beach Community Church, a.k.a. Beach Church, gratefully fulfilling the Kingdom purpose on my life as a pastoral counselor and licensed and ordained Chaplain.

God's call on my life has provided the stability we needed as a family and a consistent outlet for my passion to teach and mentor others in the teachings of Jesus Christ through God's Word. I am passionate about helping hurting people heal and thrive. I have even had the privilege to travel to India with a small team of other teachers and pastors to teach and train pastors and missionaries. I am fulfilling Christ's commission in Matthew 28:18, The Great Commission, to make disciples as I train, teach, and baptize them in the name of the Father, Son, and Holy Spirit.

It will suffice to know that over the years, we went to ballfields, dance classes, karate, gymnastics, and all school events.

We were grafted into a body of Believers through our church and in our community who love one another and loved on us. I saw God show off as He provided excellent educations, summer camp at Ridgecrest every year, school activities and trips, abundant Christmases, great friends, and lots of prayers. Both Julie and Benjamin have their own *God Stories* of how He provided each one of them with a car through high school, along with their college scholarships.

The summer of 2014 brought many changes for our family, so we went back to our beautiful Blue Ridge Mountains for a vacation. Benjamin was heading into the Army and an empty nest was on my horizon. I didn't know when we would all be able to be together again.

My plan was simple. Julie and her husband, Tripp, Benjamin and his fiance, Chelsea, and I would all stay in a picturesque chalet on the side of Beech Mountain. We had plans to go white water rafting, hike mountain trails, and fish in the streams. We would visit Grandfather Mountain and Linville Caverns and anywhere else the *kids* would decide to go. But, of course, I knew we would also go to the breathtaking knoll that cradled the *earth suits* of our precious loved ones. In fact, I had decided that we would do that on the first day of our time in our beloved mountains.

We all enjoyed sleeping in that first morning and eating a leisurely breakfast above the clouds. After all, we weren't on the clock this week. By mid-day, the sky was stunningly bright and clear, no clouds in the sky, and the summer greens on the trees were welcoming as we piled into one car and headed over to the sacred cemetery hill about twenty minutes away. My desire was to simply speak God's promises and blessings over my dear children. In the Old Testament, parents often spoke blessings over their children and God had impressed on my heart the desire to do the same. Before I had left home, I wrote out what I wanted to say. I made a small booklet for each of them with my words of blessing to capture this moment in time. I had also brought a whimsically painted metal bird with large open wings to place between the graves to symbolize the releasing of our children to fly. I affectionately called this special time, "The Celebration of Wings," and let them know that this was the only thing I had on my agenda. Everything else they could schedule at will.

They were happy to accommodate me. We soon reached the secluded country road that led up to the railroad crossing and further up to the graves. As we parked the car and walked over to the graves, a loud long train whistle sounded from across the Cove, and we began to hear the rhythmic approach of the locomotive coming around the loop. Julie and I exchanged looks of incredulity as our eyes filled with tears. God was right here with us! He met us, once again, on our beloved hill! Another divine appointment! Once again, He would show us He was with us, and I believe He brought our beloved others to bear witness. They were watching through a timeless portal from above. We weren't with them yet, but somehow, they were with us.

On this day we would *Celebrate Wings* as I released my children to live in God's plan and purpose for their lives! Thank you, Heavenly Father, for Your presence and blessings over my family. Your love is with us and will sustain us to infinity and beyond!

*"If I rise on the wings of the dawn,
if I settle on the far side of the sea,
even there Your hand will guide
me; Your right hand will hold me
fast."*
Psalm 139:9-10 (NIV)

Epilogue: With Job

"The Lord blessed the latter part of Job's life more than the

first...."

Job 42:12 (NIV)

Time has passed swiftly through these years. I survived the empty nest season when my children left home by focusing on the inner call of my life in ministry through the local church. I have served at Beach Church for over twenty years where only God can number the spiritual sons and daughters I have taught, discipled, and touched in some small way as they have experienced transformation and healing through my classes and pastoral counseling. I am continuously motivated to introduce others to experience Christ and to model how GOD IS BIGGER. I believe that they can also be *overcomers* of this broken world, not only survivors. No matter whatever comes their way, they can still experience the strength the JOY of the LORD will give them.

I reflect on one of the pivotal visitations from God that I experienced. The night of Will's death with the living picture and message from Father God comes to my mind as sharp in my memory as the night it was received. When God said, "Daughter, I AM BIGGER" and "REMEMBER JOB" it would be indelibly scribed and marked upon my life.

It would surely take time and intentionality for me to look at things through an eternal lens. I know my experience in heaven initially helped with that, but I would struggle with my own faith and belief in a loving God and not the punishing God of my childhood and immaturity. My faith and belief in God as being love was modeled by others who I looked up to within the body of Christ. Yet, what I knew and experienced with God was often very different from the world that I lived in. I have been on a quest to know the One, True, Holy Living God. Traditions, ideologies, banal thoughts, and excesses within our culture seem so trivial compared to the teachings of Christ His only Son. His teaching through the Bible was *simple*: Love the LORD with all your heart, soul, mind, and strength. Then love others as you love yourself, but it was *not easy*. God always knows your true motives for every action you take. I barely knew myself and who my Creator made me to be and what He purposed my life to be.

In our English language, we use two words: simple and easy. Their meanings interchangeably are used at times, but they are actually very different. *Simple* does not mean easy when it comes to doing something, for example pulling weeds out from around your plants is a simple task, yet, *not easy* because it can be backbreaking and tedious, long, and hard work.

Coming back from the depths of such sorrow and suffering would be like that for me as I am now sure it was for Job. I have read and reread different versions and commentaries of the Holy Bible, and I've come to an even greater peace for my own days ahead in this season of my life. These years of intentionally looking into the unseen and trying to see and hear God's perspective through His Word on my own challenges and losses have shaped me. His Word through its promises and revelation have rebuilt me and grown me as well as it has strengthened me. My simple faith has become strong!

I believe as we learn about Job's life and losses, we see that we can relate in our humanness in all the areas of life in which we are tested. Spiritually, intellectually, emotionally, relationally, financially, and even physically God of Jehovah knows all the areas in which to refine us best. It is in His creative power through our lives that we are empowered supernaturally when we choose His ways that are not our ways. Even though Job did not actually have a choice in the events that were ahead for him, God knew he was ready for the test because Job had been prepared by the hand of God. Job knew that all he possessed was God's. God knew Job trusted Him no matter what. Job was a man of integrity.

Job's relationship with God was an intimate one. Satan hated the beautiful picture of unity and oneness and wanted to destroy it. It was for that very reason Satan wanted to take away from Job that security that was there deep inside of Job's character. God was fully confident in Job's integrity. God knew Job's heart better than anyone. God knew Job loved Him even more than all the many gifts God had given him. An intimate relationship with God is still the strongest bond in the universe, and God is still actively seeking those in this world who will love Him with all they are and all they have. This is how our relationship becomes bigger, deeper, and eternally minded, even as we are challenged by the losses of all we hold dear to us. You never really lose anything that you have already given back to God; that is how knowing and belief in God is always working for us and not against us.

As much as I have learned over these years while serving Him, one of my biggest challenges has been understanding and reconciling the violent death of a child. How does God restore or redeem what has been prematurely or senselessly taken in this dark world? I guess the short answer is He promises to make all things new one day, which births another question. So, as a believer in God, do I have to die to be happy?

In the last chapter of the book of Job, at first look, we see abundance, healing, and joy again. Blessings that were wiped out in a moment now are returned at the deep and personal cost of suffering, anguish, waiting, and continued walking and testing without any mention of the possibility of more loss in the future. So, it has been for me.

****

So, does my story parallel that of Job's? On the day when we stood on the knoll at the graves and felt the presence of our loved ones -- that beautiful day when I released and blessed my children with our 2014 *Celebration of Wings* ceremony -- there was a new little life present that day. He was snuggled safe under Julie's heart and in her womb, in the *Secret Place*. God would begin to grow our family again, and I would discover a depth of love I never knew was there. I would become a Nona (Italian for Grandmother) and for the first time. In many years, a new life was being added to my family.

As I approach the holidays every year, dark thoughts try to invade as the leaves begin to fall, and my spirits begin to drop. Once again, another fall season is coming around quickly and ushering in the holidays. The date of Will's murder on November 5 and his birthday being December 5, along with the Thanksgiving sandwich and Christmas dessert seems almost too much to bear with every passing year.

We tried to do things that helped ease the loss of vacant chairs during the holidays. We would cut down our Christmas tree at Thanksgiving and decorate it on December 5. That became the *new normal* tradition, but once Bill died and the children grew up, more loss piled on top of loss, so I just clung tighter to Jesus and did my best to stay busy to make it through. Most times it was one day at a time and sometimes one moment at a time. I would call out to God. *Do I have to wait until I'm in heaven to have this void in my heart filled? How can you make this right?* Honestly, some days the loss of a child seems to be a forever scar with a seeping wound.

In our post pandemic world today, many may want to forget Christmas 2020 for a myriad of reasons. But I will end this story now to tell you about the Stapleton Supernatural Christmas Celebration of 2020. It was truly a miracle conceived in Heaven.

I guess I should start with two weeks before the world shut down. I did take a bad fall, landing flat on my face and breaking both of my arms and some teeth. I felt so helpless. It was embarrassing, as well. I fell right in front of a crowd of people at a state park. You know that expression, "Go big or go home," right? Well, I ended up in the emergency room, never dreaming that the rest of the world would be joining me shortly in quarantine for COVID-19.

My surgery for the broken bones was among the last done at the surgical center before it was closed by the pandemic. It not only planted me at home and shifted my job to videoconferencing, which has been a huge blessing, but it kept all of us from traveling. I wasn't allowed or able to drive anyway. Both Julie and Benjamin and their families live significant distances away from me and each other. For Christmas of 2020, Benjamin and his wife, Chelsea, were stationed in a military base, just a few states away, so we all were kept apart through Covid.

I missed them terribly, but we talked often, and *face timed* regularly. In the spring of 2020, Ben and Chelsea announced the

good news. Little Ellie was going to be a big sister; we all were thrilled! This baby would bless Nona with five grandchildren in five years! Aaron had been joined by Selah and Johnny by now. They are all known collectively and affectionately as "Nona's Ninjas," and each one has stealthily taken over every part of my heart!

As I began to pray for this new little life being knit together in Chelsea's womb. I couldn't help but think about the due date Chelsea's doctor had predicted -- "Mid December, actually the 17th." I immediately thought, *Wow! Lord, really? Do you think this baby could be born on the fifth? Please, Lord, you know little Will's birthday was one of the happiest days of my life. He made me a mommy, but it's been the saddest day on the calendar ever since he left. Lord, will you restore that joy of life to me and make this a joyously celebrated birthday again?*

At that time, we didn't even know whether it was a boy or a girl. I just knew I wanted the saddest day on my calendar to be redeemed with the joy that only God, our Creator, would be able to do. With each day of anticipation, I would have a deep peace as I was healing from my arm surgeries for the baby to be born on December 5th. As I look back now, I really was like a little child not wanting to let go of a piece of candy. I wanted this so bad! Then, the ultra-sound picture came in to show the baby was indeed a little boy. He was growing beautifully. Even though there was no wavering on a due date, I felt like God, and I had a special bond of understanding, and He was going to do this for me. However, my dear little Chelsea, my daughter-in-love, wasn't quite as confident, but I knew she wanted to believe me. So, I tried to assure her that I just wanted her and the baby to be healthy. God already knew every day before one of them came to be. God and I had a tight bond, and I was not letting go. After all, there was no *plan B.*

I still couldn't drive a car because of my arm injuries, so as the holidays neared, we began to put some plans and some prayers into place. One of my *dear spiritual daughters*, Ruthie, who is a registered nurse and travel nurse, committed to drive me to Ben and Chelsea's for the holidays. We sang Christmas songs as we traveled and arrived in full Christmas Spirit on the evening of December 3, 2020. Poor Chelsea, she had been to the doctor earlier, but the doctor wouldn't say one way or the other. Just the fact that the doctor didn't say, "I'll see you next week," was a comfort and a "yes" and "amen" for this Nona! So, I stayed strong in my faith and trust in the God Who was going to do something great!

I even tried to set Chelsea's mind at ease the next day by telling her the story of Julie's birth and how this situation reminded me of my own mother who had come a long way by train to be with me. We had gone to church, and an obstetric (OB) nurse took one look at me in the church lobby and said, "Oh, you've got at least another week or so." I was so discouraged, crushed, and frustrated as I thought about my mother's time and schedule. The prospect of waiting any longer just put more pressure on me. Frankly, it made me angry and sick at the same time. After all, what can you really do? Babies come in God's timing, of course. We'll make this long story short by telling you that Baby Julie was born the very next day!

I shared that with Chelsea, but she was understandably stressed and deservedly cranky! Ben took me aside late on the evening of the fourth. He said, "Don't worry Mom; she was the same way right before Ellie came. We all said our "good nights" and agreed that if they had to go to the hospital during the night, they would let me know, so Ruthie and I could be on alert for Ellie. Sure enough, at about 2:00 a.m., I was awakened by a text from Benjamin, informing me that Chelsea's water broke at midnight, her contractions were increasing, and they were heading to the hospital.

William Thomas Stapleton was born healthy and on God time at 1:04 p.m. December 5, 2020. This was our families' Christmas Miracle! Of course, we know God knew all along. OUR HEAVENLY FATHER placed that seed breathing life into this new little Will, and he arrived in God's impeccable timing! Huge healing hugs and kisses filled our souls from heaven! This was God's answer to fervent prayers of tested faith and thanksgiving for all HIS amazing blessings.

Tripp and Julie, with the other three Ninjas, journeyed to join us for the Christmas Celebration of our dear Savior's birth, and of course, Nona, along with all her Ninjas, had the best Christmas ever!

"I will utter hidden things, things from old – things we have heard and known, things our ancestors have told us. We will not hide them from their descendants; we will tell the next generation the praise worthy deeds of the Lord, his power, and the wonders he has done."
Psalm 78:1-4 (KJV)

Family Christmas 2020

Works Cited

Chambers, Oswald. *My Utmost for His Highest,* edited by James Reimann, Dodd, Mead & Co, 1925.

Crouch, Andrew Edward. "Through it All." *Day One.* 2015.

Feeley, Jef. "Teen Will Testify for Prosecution: Charge Reduced in Boy's Death." *The Columbia Record.* 1987 January 21. pp. 1-A, 9-A.

Feeley, Jef. "Prosecutor Closes with Charges of Malice. *The Columbia Record.* 1987 January 21. pp. 1-A, 5-A.

Hamilton, Ron. "Oh Rejoice in the Lord." 2022. www.gccsatx.com.

Hook, Steve. "Boulder Kills Boy: Two-year-old Dies When Rock Dropped from Bridge Hits Car." *The State.* 1986 November 6. pp.1-A, 4-A.

Hook, Steve. "Mother Says Family Stronger After Tragedy." *The State.* 1986 December 5. pp.1-A, 11-A.

Kushin, Phil. "A Family Ordeal." *Potential.* 1987 November/December. pp. 10-11.

Libby, Larry and Wayne McLoughlin (Illus.). *Someday Heaven.* Zonderkids. 2001.

Martin, Civilla. "Be Not Dismayed Whate'er Betide." *John A. Davis' Songs of Redemption and Praise.* 1905

McInerney, Salley. "Cola Town." *The Columbia Record.* 1986 November 13.

Moen, Don. *Worship with Don Moen.* "God Will Make a Way." 2008

Nelson, Rick. "'Word of God' Helps Sustain Family After Child's Tragic Death." *The Evening Post.* 1987 February 5. *p.* 1-B – 2B.

"North Cove Folks Wonderful." *The McDowell News.* 1987 February 19. p. 4.

O'Boyle, Peter III. "Death scene visited: Suspects' accounts of 'stoning' conflict." *The State.* 1987 January 21. pp.1- A, 14-A.

O'Boyle, Peter III. "Victim's father testifies: Impact of deadly rock was like hitting a wall." *The State.* 1987 January 20. pp.1-C, 4-C.

O'Boyle, Peter III. "Teen guilty in boulder death." *The State.* 1987 January 22. p. A-1.

"Officials seek preventive measures." *The Dispatch News.* 1986 November 12, p.1.

Smyth, Dolores. "Why Was Lucifer, Satan, Cast Out of Heaven and Banished to Hell?" www.*Christianity.com.* · 2020 October 12.

More About the Author: Linda Toro Stapleton

Linda is passionate about pouring out her heart and pointing many to Jesus. She has been in His service for most of her adult life. She has an education background and her master's degree in Biblical Counseling.

Linda has served as a Director of Care Ministry, a pastoral counselor, and taught Biblical Discipleship at Myrtle Beach Community Church a.k.a. Beach Church for the past twenty-five years. She has maintained a close relationship with Victorious Christian Living International (VCLI) and has faithfully used the SALT (Seven Areas of Life Training) Discipleship Tools to teach and equip the church body. Linda is a gifted, as well as a licensed and ordained Senior Chaplain with a long-standing association with the IFOC (International Fellowship of Chaplains) and serves her local chapter as a Chaplain of Chaplains. Through her teaching and counseling of countless men and women in their pain and challenges in life, she has been a faithful conduit of wisdom, healing, and comfort through God's power.

Linda has spoken at many conferences, women's groups, and graciously received an honorary doctorate when she taught pastors and missionaries with GTSSS (Gospel Tribal Society of Social Services) in India – through (VCLI).

Her favorite people call her "Nona," which is Italian for grandmother, and she cheekily refers to her grandchildren as "Nona's Ninjas." Her constant companion is Chief, a Whippador, who always wears a bowtie and thinks he is a person. She loves her family deeply, is inspired by sunrises, flowers in her garden, and people who don't give up. She is an insatiable reader and learner and loves to walk on the beach and listen to His voice.

Linda believes that tragedy does not shape who you become; it reveals who you are. During her life, she has always loved to write and journal but only for her own sanity and healing. She told God she would not write the story until He gave her the title, which He did through a vision in 2008. She wrote the story, shared pieces of it through speaking and teaching, raised her children, and put the story on a shelf for her family. Then one day, a dear friend asked if she could read it. Her friend then took it to her friend, Sandi, an author and new publisher.

We all believe *Above the Overpass* was written for "such a time as this."

Linda and her beloved friend, Chief.

"Your love witnesses more than one thousand sermons."

His Honorable Hubert E. Long,

Presiding Judge

Reviews and Endorsements

Have you ever set down to select a good book or wanted to be swept away into a world of intrigue, especially if it's a true story? I know I have, but it's never easy to find, is it? Well take heart; when I read this book, I was blown away! When I finished this book, I just sat and stared at the last page. Let that sink in a minute. This is an astonishingly well-written account of God's handiwork and Satan's attempt to destroy it.

Over thirteen years have passed since I first watched Linda Stapleton use her soft but powerful words to captivate a large audience. She was speaking in the sanctuary of the church where she has served humbly for over twenty-five years as a teaching counselor. This woman's faith is rooted in her love for Jesus, the scriptures, and the power of the Holy Spirit. Her uncanny ability to hear from God is as much a part of her as is her long ponytail that is always caught up in a loose bun. You will want to spend your days and evenings with her as you read this vivid account of how God wove a beautiful tapestry of good into her life out of what the enemy meant for evil.

Enjoy the warmth and comfort as she shepherds you into your own closer walk with Jesus. You will witness first-hand her nightmares, her miraculous dreams, the visitations, transportations, and the extraordinary visions manifested through her faith in Jesus Christ. See for yourself how His control of everyday situations can mean all the diffrence and everything. Born out of tragedy, destined for eternity, you will never forget her powerful story. "You intended to harm me, but God intended it for good to accomplish what is now being done, the saving of many lives."

Gloria Kasler, RN/Administrator/CEO
Nightingale's Nursing & Attendants

****

Linda has been developing this book for many years, and I have been honored to have read some of the drafts. While reading, I get so emotionally moved to the point of tears and admiration for what God has done through Linda to hone her into a spiritual warrior.

I met Linda about seven years ago and learned early on about her amazing spiritual insightful abilities. Her background, intelligence, and loving heart make up the solid spiritual foundation from which God has worked to affect people who have affected other people in a fruitful way.

The book, *Above the Overpass,* is captivating and intriguing, so captivating I did not want to put the book down even though my emotions were so affected. It was intriguing because of the tragic circumstances, spiritual challenges, and personal functionality that Linda and her family endured.

Linda's encouragement is the reason I became a chaplain. She indicated she was an ordained chaplain with the International Fellowship of Chaplains, and she thought the training would be beneficial in my calling to serve and care for others for God's purpose. By following through with her encouragement, God has blessed many of us.

We now have our own Corp of Chaplains in Myrtle Beach

known as the I.F.O.C. Carolina Coastal Chaplain Corps. We are about twenty-five chaplains strong serving our Lord. Linda has been a chaplain of the I.F.O.C. for fifteen years. I have Linda honored as our Chaplain of Chaplains for our Corps.

I highly recommend this potentially life-changing book to anyone who wants to explore the workings of God in our lives through tragedy, pain, and heartache. In my opinion, it is a must read. In sincere appreciation to Linda Toro Stapleton for who you are and the love you show to others, I am

Captain James C. Wilmot
I.F.O.C. Carolina Coastal Chaplain Corps Commander
chaplainjames19@gmail.com

****

Above the Overpass is a compelling story of one person's journey through life. The descriptive details written by the author walked me through her losses, heartbreaks, and forgiveness in her life.

From the beginning chapter to the end chapter, she shares with the reader that God is bigger through it all. It brought to my mind a favorite song, "Through It All" (Crouch).

Above the Overpass is a must read and one to share!

Dr. Suzanne L'Amoreaux
Victorious Christian Living, Int.

For the past eight years, I've worked alongside Linda Stapleton as she directed the Care Ministry of Beach Church. I have witnessed her care and compassion firsthand. Linda gives selflessly to others and has great empathy towards them. These God-given characteristics carry over into her daily pastoral counseling sessions. With over twenty-plus years of experience and ministering to the brokenhearted, her expertise is well documented.

This loving side of Linda spills into the story within the pages of *Above the Overpass*. The book clearly demonstrates the love of God through a genuine tale of pain and heartache that only a mother can express when losing a child. Sharing her story of unimaginable loss allows the reader to walk through her tribulation step by step. We feel the overwhelming pain and the "Why me?" moments right alongside her. Through beautifully written prose, Linda has captured the challenges of staying close to God when plunged head on into a heartbreaking situation.

Above the Overpass is a real page turner. I seriously could not put the book down!

Judy Wilmot
Founder and Director of
Agape Love Box Ministry Myrtle Beach

Honored to have known Linda and her children for many years and having been impacted by her incredible courage, I am grateful God has called Linda to share her family's gripping and tragic story.

Linda's genuine faith in and love for the Lord can be found in every heartfelt word. Written as if you are walking the journey with her, the reader is sure to experience the gut-wrenching emotion and strength of faith that truly surpasses human understanding. Woven with scripture, Linda's story demonstrates just how big, faithful, and sovereign our Heavenly Father is.

This is a story of assurance that He loves us more than we can comprehend and that we are truly never alone. *Above the Overpass* -- I believe with all my heart this story will inspire and encourage many for years to come. How such devastation can be recounted with all paths leading back to our loving Heavenly Father and to inconceivable forgiveness is a testament to both Linda's beauty and brilliance.

Lovingly submitted, I am

Nancy Henry
Administrator Emeritus
Christian Academy of Myrtle Beach
Nhenry@christianacademysaints.org

When I received the draft of Linda Stapleton's book, *Above the Overpass*, and was asked to read and review it, I did not anticipate the emotional rollercoaster ride I was about to undertake! This book brought me to tears and laughter, anger and shame, love and hate, but the most impressive part was how the family, ultimately, turn to God. One thing I got out of this was how strong the Lord was in Linda's life and is even now. An old hymn came to me that describes her journey better than I can. It's "Be Not Dismayed Whate'er Betide" (Martin). Linda and her family lived the words of this old hymn.

I wholeheartedly recommend this amazing book as one that should be in every Christian's library.

Dr. Ray L'Amoreaux
CEO and President of Victorious Christian Living
International
www.Vcli.org

****

Linda's writing makes you feel as if you are a shadow trailing alongside her, witnessing every scene as it unfolds.

You won't be able to put it down, and you will be changed forever. We believe that the Holy Spirit will catapult you into the sacred spaces of every reader's heart.

There are some stories that just need to be shared. This is one of them.

Gary and Kelli Wadsten
The Wadsten Group
kkwadsten@aol.com

The moments and events in our lives weave a story that has the power to impact us and have an even greater power to impact others. As a pastor for over thirty years, I understand many times tragic events define us in a way that we never recover. In this book, you will discover that even in your darkest hour, God is always present, and He can handle what you want to escape.

Linda's honesty and ability to share an encounter no one ever wishes to experience draws you in and allows you to feel how desperate and alone we can be, where our world is lived in our thoughts, numb to the reality of our situation.

Yet, as I've witnessed while we have served together in ministry, Linda has determined that God is BIGGER and His arms wider, and He invites us to rest in Him. I highly recommend you take a moment to read her incredible story, as you again discover and grasp *"how wide, how long, how high, and how deep His love is"* (Ephesians 3:18).

Damon Adcock
Chief Culture Officer
Pyle Financial Services
damonadcock@gmail.com

Linda Stapleton is a remarkable woman of incredible faith. Few people I know have experienced the depth of pain and heartbreak tht she has, yet through it all, Linda has continually found her strength in the presence of the Savior.

Her story of brokenness and victory has moved many to pursue the joy of forgiveness. I'm so thankful for her courage and boldness to share with us this journey God has brought her through.

I'm looking forward to seeing how God uses this story to bring healing to so many who have been bound by the pain of their past.

Greg Anderson
Fellowship of Christian Athletes
Palm Beach County
Metro-Director
GAnderson@FCA.org
www.FCApbc.org

A Note to My Readers

Out of all the millions of books in this world, you are holding my life story in your hands. Thank you for even considering to read it. I truly hope you enjoyed it. It is all true and from my perspective on actual events. This is a genuine story of Job and how God made impossible things possible and ordinary events extraordinary. I believe God called me to a suffering that many will never understand.

After sharing bits and pieces with others, I would continually hear from those around me, "You should write a book." I didn't take it seriously at first, but I told the Lord if He wanted me to write it, then He would have to give me a title. He is the One who not only gave me the title, but delivered it to me as a picture in my mind's eye. This is the story He wrote on my life.

Only the One who created me knew this day of birthing His story into print would come true. He gets all the glory for *"snatching me out of the mirey clay and planting my feet on the rock of my salvation."* (Paraphrased from Psalm 40: 2, NIV.) My Jesus, I give Him the Glory, great things he has done!

There were many supporting cast members in my story. You met them throughout these pages. I am so grateful for their presence in my life. Each chapter is entitled as an attribute of God revealed within the chapter. You are able to see it more clearly looking back.

Acknowledgements

"You shall love the Lord your God with all your heart and with all your soul and with all your mind. This is the great and first commandment. And the second is like it: You shall love your neighbor as yourself. On these two commandments depend on all the Law and the Prophets."

Matthew 22:37- 40 (ESV)

This story cannot be told without the real names, hearts, and actions of the people who touched our lives. You know who you are.

You reached in and loved us with open hands and hearts. You helped a fellow human being, and God saw you. Our gratefulness is beyond words. On this side of life, we hope to pay it forward. On the other side of this life, we'll have eternity to share precious memories and personally hug and show you how grateful we will always be.

We have all been created to love one another.

Available at
Here I Am Publishing, LLC

Sunsets After the Storms (Kilgore)

Above the Overpass (Stapleton)

Richard's Key Roy's Sandman (Edwards)

Three Day Nights (Edwards)

The Clumsy Little Angel (Edwards)

All for Him (Barnes)

Silent Victims Devotional (Barnes)

Hands Reaching, Hearts Touching Devotional (Barnes)

The Good Sheriff (Good)

You Can't Kill the Miracle (Torres)

God's Hands (Jarrett)

A Melody Too Sweet to Forget (DeSilva)

Go to www.hereiampublishingllc.com

CPSIA information can be obtained
at www.ICGtesting.com
Printed in the USA
LVHW051235250123
737906LV00003B/42